Bernese Alps
Western Touring Route

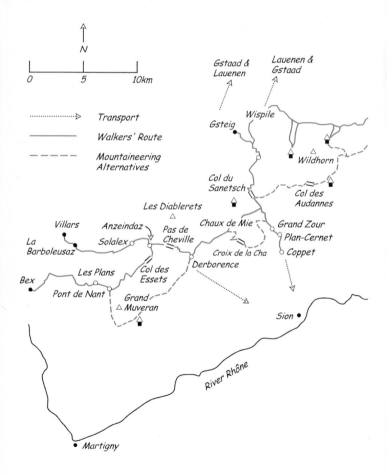

Pernese Alps
\ /estern
T uring Route

cordee

Text, photographs and maps © Geoffrey Pocock 2005

Dedication
For Jeremy Naish who loved the mountains

First edition 2005

Published by Cordee Ltd, 3a de Montfort Street,
Leicester LE1 7HD, England

Printed in Italy

ISBN 1 904207 25 1

A catalogue record for this book is available from the British Library

Editorial, design and production management by Outcrop Publishing
Services Ltd, Cumbria

The contents of this book were believed to be correct at the time of
printing. Nevertheless, the author, the publishers and their agents
cannot be held resposible for any errors or ommissions, or for
changes in the details given in this book, or for the consequences of
any reliance on the information it provides. This does not affect your
statutory rights. We have made every effort to ensure the accuracy of
this guide but the landscape is always changing so we welcome any
feedback readers may have. Email your comments to
info@cordee.co.uk.

For maps and other guides to Switzerland and the rest of the world
visit www.cordee.co.uk.

Bernese Alps
Western
Touring Route

Geoffrey Pocock

cordee

Contents

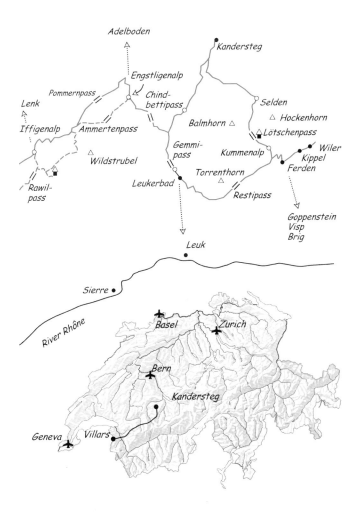

Symbols and Abbreviations

●	Hotels
○	Mountain inn
⌂	Mountain hut, SAC or private
▪◆	Hamlet or isolated buildings
☦	Church or chapel
─△	Ridge and peak
✗	Spot height
═════	Metalled road
─────	Jeep track
··············	Footpath
▭▭▭▭▭▭	Railway
◀─ ─ ─▶	Cable-car or gondola
LK	Landeskarte der Schweiz (Swiss federal map)
SAC	Swiss Alpine Club
H.	Hut
Cab.	Cabane

Foreword

The watershed separating the cantons Berne and Valais starts in the Canton Vaud at the massif of Les Diablerets and runs north-east, in much the same direction as the Rhône Valley, embracing the Wildhorn, the Wildstrubel and the Balmhorn. This is high Alpine terrain with glaciers and snow-clad peaks to challenge the Alpinist, but it is also a delightful area for the walker.

One of the earliest descriptions of walking in this region is to be found in Ball's *Alpine Guide – The Central Alps* (1864). Ball describes a variety of passages to the north and south of the ridge as well as a high level route taking in a number of peaks. A few years later, in 1894, Conway recorded his exploration of some of the route in his classic book, *The Alps from End to End*. He would have completed the route south of the main ridge if the exigencies of journalism had not deflected him from Leukerbad to the Pennine Alps instead of continuing to the Lötschental. For decades after these early walking tours much of the route has been followed as a ski tour, but in 1970 Collomb, in his guide *Bernese Alps West*, reintroduced the idea of a long-distance walk through these mountains. Since then the increasing popularity of mountain walking has led the Swiss to improve many of the paths that form the route.

This book describes a walking tour from Villars to Kandersteg, which crosses high cols from one mountain inn or village to the next; at a leisurely pace it will take about two weeks. It is aimed at walkers who wish to enjoy a holiday with comfortable accommodation and good food. It will, however, be equally valuable to those who prefer huts to hotels or inns and they will find that the standard of accommodation and food in mountain huts, SAC as well as private, is extremely good nowadays. One way or another – perhaps balancing nights spent in the mountains with those in a village – this tour offers the prospect of a most enjoyable holiday.

Acknowledgement

I am indebted to Robin Collomb who suggested this route to me. Thanks are also due to Pam Collomb and my wife, Anne Davis, who joined me for some of the exploration.

Introduction

Walking in the Alps

I am aware that, whilst many people who might buy this guidebook will be experienced Alpine walkers, some may not have tackled an Alpine pass in their lives. If you have never walked in the Alps you may be uncertain about your ability to undertake this tour and what you might be faced with. In normal conditions, most walking in the Alps is no more demanding than walking in Britain: the weather is generally much better, the paths are well marked and the gradients not too severe. Anyone who is an experienced hill walker and can spend a day in the British hills, climbing a few peaks and navigating in poor conditions, is more than able to tackle this tour. To satisfy walkers of all abilities the tour is described in two sections.

The first section covers the complete tour from Villars to Kandersteg and is aimed at the hill walker who prefers to spend as much time as possible on footpaths with grass and wild flowers to each side. The accommodation available is mainly mountain inns rather than huts and, at the end of almost every day's walking, there is good transport to a nearby village with hotels and shops.

The second section suggests some alternative, more difficult stages, that should appeal to experienced Alpine walkers who prefer mountain huts and inns to hotels and seek challenging routes over high and rugged passes. These are referred to as Mountaineering Alternatives but they do not require any specialised equipment, although an ice-axe could be useful in the early season and a mixed party might carry a rope. Walkers used to high mountain terrain, with a good head for heights and the ability to move confidently on snow, will find several routes that should satisfy their more ambitious expectations. They will find plenty of accommodation to allow them to go on foot the whole way without passing a night in a village.

Of course, there is nothing to stop you making your way by a combination of routes from the two sections, alternating nights spent in huts or inns with a day off in a village and a night in a hotel. Some people may wish to omit part of the route altogether and use public transport instead. Details of suitable buses and cable-cars are included in Appendix C. Finally, a third section describing a number of day walks is included. These offer the opportunity of getting into the mountains with a light rucksack and no pressure to get to the next hotel or hut.

When to go

In the high Alps, the summer season is short: from the end of June to mid-September, but for the routes described here any time between mid-June and late September or even early October should afford pleasant weather and good conditions. At the end of June and the beginning of July, it is not too busy and the Alpine flowers are at their best but there may still be a great deal of snow to clear, particularly after a good winter for skiing. The busiest time is between the second week of July and the third week of August, especially at weekends, and where accommodation is limited it may be difficult to obtain. However, the higher passes are less likely to be snowy and, if bad weather occurs, the days are warm enough to melt new snow very quickly. Towards the beginning of September the crowds start to disappear, making the paths much more enjoyable and accommodation easier to find. However, bad weather can put down sufficient snow to make things awkward for several days. Also, some seasonal transport stops running after the middle of September. On balance, the cooler weather and lack of crowds make the end of the season the best compromise.

How to get there and back

Switzerland is easily reached by road, rail or air. A great deal of general information is available on the internet from the Switzerland Tourism website, www.myswitzerland.com, and many other sites provide additional detail and timetables for all modes of travel. It is easy to make all the reservations on the internet but, if a traditional approach is preferred, bookings can be made through Plus Travel who operate on behalf of the Swiss Tourist Office. Important addresses are given at end of this section.

Not so long ago it was taken for granted that travel by car to the Alps was the least expensive way for a party of three or four people, but the development of low-cost airlines has made travelling to Switzerland very easy and inexpensive and it is now probably the preferred method. Services to Switzerland are operated by several airlines from a number of airports in the UK and Ireland. The best point of arrival is Geneva. The railway station is in the airport terminal and Villars is easily reached by train in about 2½ hours. For the train journey buy a Swiss Transfer Ticket, which is valid for one journey from the Swiss border to your destination and back. This cannot be bought in Switzerland but must be purchased before leaving the UK from Plus Travel (or its equivalent in other countries). Using a Swiss Transfer Ticket, other airports, such as Zürich, Bern or Basel, could be used with a longer transfer by rail but at no additional expense. Getting back to Geneva from Kandersteg presents no problems, with hourly trains and a journey of about 3½ hours.

Travelling to the Alps by car naturally takes longer than flying but for a large party might be less expensive. Visitors can take a private car into Switzerland for a temporary stay without customs documents, provided a valid national driving licence and the vehicle registration certificate can be produced. All United Kingdom and Republic of Ireland motor insurance policies provide the minimum legal cover required by EU countries and Switzerland, so a Green Card is not compulsory. However, as the cover provided is limited, motorists are strongly advised before any trip abroad to obtain a Green Card from their insurers, to provide the same cover they enjoy when driving in the UK.

A permit is needed for cars and motorcycles and an additional fee applies to trailers and caravans, otherwise there are no tolls. The permit costs about £20 and can be bought at the border crossing or from Plus Travel. Vehicles with a weight of more than 3.5 tonnes – this includes camper vans – have to pay a heavy-goods road tax at the border on entry into Switzerland.

If you spend a night or two in Villars before starting it may be possible to leave the car in your hotel car park, otherwise there is plenty of public parking but the local police should be advised of a long stay. They can be contacted by fax on 00 41 24 496 33 15. At the end of the holiday it is easy to get back to your car from Kandersteg by public transport, hourly trains taking about 3 hours.

Travel by train is best suited to those living in the south of England and can become rather expensive. An early morning Eurostar from London to Paris arrives in sufficient time for lunch at the elegant restaurant Le Train Bleu, at the Gare de Lyon, before taking the TGV to Geneva from where there are frequent trains to Bex via Lausanne and good connections to Villars. The cheapest ticket combination is a 14-day apex return on Eurostar, a return on the TGV and a Swiss Transfer Ticket. If you do not want to be constrained by a return date Eurostar has different types of flexible tickets and it is easy to buy a ticket to Paris the day before the return. But a note of caution – the TGV can be fully booked at weekends and recently there have been long queues at the Gare du Nord for passengers changing reservations with standard class flexible tickets.

At the time of writing Eurostar is operating a strict security regime and passengers are not allowed to carry dangerous items such as penknives, ice-axes or crampons. These must be taken to the Euro-Dispatch Centre at Waterloo an hour before departure and sent as registered luggage. They can be collected at the Gare du Nord about 30 minutes after arrival.

Accommodation

The style of accommodation available in the Alps varies with altitude: hotels in the valleys, mountain inns on summer pastures and huts in isolated mountainous areas. Mountain inns offer a good compromise between the luxury, but expense, of hotels and the very simple facilities available in huts. Most mountain inns have a number of small rooms as well as dormitory accommodation and many have hot showers, although en-suite facilities are relatively rare. They provide a substantial evening meal and are good value for money. Mountain huts, whether private or SAC, normally have only dormitory accommodation. Blankets are provided so a sleeping bag is not necessary but a sheet sleeping bag makes the bed more comfortable; a silk liner is bliss and weighs a lot less than cotton. Usually the facilities are simple but hardened mountaineers of the old school should be prepared for some shocks – a shower in the Lötschenpass Hut for example.

In any of the villages – Gsteig, Lenk etc – you will find a selection of hotels at a price and level of quality to suit most tastes. These villages also have banks and shops and, some, even swimming pools to add to the pleasure of the walk. A list of hotels, inns and huts is given in Appendix A.

What to take

Take as little as possible, but enough to cater for all possibilities of weather, accommodation and changes of plan. It should be possible to get away without an ice-axe, even at the end of the season, but it would be advisable to take one in late June or early July, especially if you wish to try some of the mountaineering alternatives.

To keep the weight down a parcel of clean clothes can be sent to a suitable village on the route; either to the post office or to a hotel if you know where you are going to stay. This can be done in Switzerland at the beginning of the walk or from the UK before you travel. Furthermore, unwanted maps, used clothes and the like, can be sent home during the course of the trip. A fuller list of suggested kit to take is set out in Appendix B.

Language

South of the watershed, in the cantons Vaud and Valais, the language spoken is French as far as Sion then German. On the north side the official language is German but almost everyone speaks French as well and most hoteliers and inn keepers also speak English. However, there might be some language difficulties in the Lötschental for non-German speakers.

Public transport

Switzerland is justifiably renowned for its public transport and this walk is well provided with connecting cable-cars, buses and trains. The times I have mentioned in the text were correct at the time of writing but they can change and should be checked before relying on them. A summary of the more useful transport options appears in Appendix C.

Money

The Swiss are keen to quote prices in Euros and, in many instances, cash payments can be made in Euros or Swiss Francs. For example, train and postbus tickets can be bought using Euros and some tele-phones are being adapted to accept Euro coins. Most hotels in the area will accept the currency but the rate of exchange is usually quite poor and it is better pay with Swiss Francs. Credit cards are generally accepted but cash is needed in the mountain huts. There are usually plenty of cash dispensers in the villages.

Insurance

Some holiday insurance policies include Alpine walking but rescue is rarely included in the cover. In the unfortunate event of needing the mountain rescue service it can be very expensive and adequate cover should be arranged before setting out. Members of the British Mountaineering Council can take advantage of the good rates offered by their insurers. Others will have to find a specialist insurer, of which there are several such as Harrison Beaumont and Snowcard.

What will it cost?

Accommodation in Switzerland is superb value for money: it is easy to find a clean, comfortable, room costing less than in the UK. For two people having dinner, bed and breakfast at a mountain inn you can expect to pay around £40 a head including drinks. Huts are less expensive, for example an overnight for two at an SAC hut will cost about £30 per person, again including drinks. In Alpine club huts there is a reduction in the price of accommodation for club members or those with reciprocal membership rights, but the difference is so small nowadays that it's not really worthwhile joining a club just for this tour.

Hotels cost more and it pays to shop around. It can be good value to stay at a modest hotel and enjoy the table d'hôte at a more expensive establishment. Outside the main part of the Alpine summer season it should be possible to get half board with a comfortable room en-suite for £45–£50 a head. Walkers used to spending a few days in a Lakeland or Scottish hotel will be delighted by the level of quality and low cost of Swiss hotels.

Maps

Four LK 1:50,000 Swiss maps – 264, 272, 273 and 5009 – cover the whole route, but the larger scale 1:25,000 maps – 1247, 1266, 1267, 1268, 1285, 1286 and 1305 – give more detail and are worth the extra weight. LK maps can be used with a GPS that has the Swiss grid as a position format and the map datum CH-1903. The sketch maps are mostly adapted from the LK 1:25,000 Swiss maps; they are intended to give an overview of the route and are not a substitute for proper maps. For clarity, rivers, cable-cars, chair-lifts etc, are only shown where they form an important feature of the route, but all can be seen on the LK maps.

Nomenclature and altitudes

Place names and altitudes are generally taken from the LK 1:25,000 maps, but I have tried not to adopt the irritating fashion currently used by the Swiss Topographical Office of omitting the letter n from some place names, for example Lötchepass instead of Lötschenpass. Names sometimes differ on 1:50,000 maps and there is often an inconsistency between maps and signposts, even with altitudes.

Timings

The times given in the route descriptions allow for short stops to check the map or take a photograph but do not take account of the need to navigate more carefully in bad weather or for proper stops for lunch. They assume that all the members of the party are fit and the route is in good condition. To instil some consistency in the timings they have been calculated using a formula based on Naismith's Rule but with corrections for steep ascents and descents and a fatigue factor at the end of the day. Because of the fatigue factor, saving time at the start of the day, by taking a bus or cable-car for example, leads to a greater saving overall.

Travel information

There is a wealth of information available from tourist offices and the internet. The following are particularly useful.

Switzerland Travel Centre Ltd
Swiss Centre, 10 Wardour Street, London W1D 6QF
tel: 00800 100 200 30
fax: 00800 100 200 31
website: www.myswitzerland.com
email: stc@stlondon.com
Can provide general information and brochures.

Plus Travel
10th Floor, Swiss Centre, 10 Wardour Street, London W1D 6QF
tel: 020 7734 0383
fax: 020 7292 1599
website: www.plustravel.co.uk
email: plustravel@stlondon.com
Offers a complete travel agent's service able to supply all tickets, motorway vignettes, and reserve accommodation.

SBB
Swiss train and postbus timetables and fare information are available
on the internet.
website: http://fahrplan.sbb.ch/bin/query.exe/en

Rail Europe Ltd
179 Piccadilly, London W1V OBA
tel: 08705 848 848
fax: 08705 717 273
website: www.raileurope.co.uk
Provides information and tickets for Eurostar and French trains
(SNCF).

SNCF
French train timetables and on-line booking are available on the
internet. This is a good service with tickets delivered to a UK address
within five working days.
website: www.sncf.com/indexe.htm

Eurostar
tel: 08705 186 186
website: www.eurostar.com
Information and tickets available by telephone or on-line.

Euro-Dispatch Centre (London Waterloo)
tel: 08705 850 850
Information on sending registered luggage ('dangerous items') on
Eurostar.

Easyjet
website: www.easyjet.com
Easyjet has regular services to Geneva from Liverpool, East Midlands,
Luton and Gatwick. Reservations must be made by internet.

Swiss – Swiss International Airlines (formerly Swissair)
tel: 0845 601 0956
website: www.swiss.com
Swiss has 42 flights a day from the UK (London City, London
Heathrow, Birmingham, Edinburgh, Manchester) to various destina-
tions in Switzerland.

British Airways
tel: 0845 773 3377
website: www.british-airways.com
BA flies to Geneva from Heathrow, Gatwick and Manchester.

Insurance
Several brokers specialise in insurance for travellers pursuing
mountain sports. I have found the following to be competitive.

British Mountaineering Council
177–179 Burton Road, Manchester M20 2BB
tel: 0161 445 4747
fax: 0161 445 4500
website: www.thebmc.co.uk
Very competitive rates for its members.

STA Travel
tel: 08701 600 599
website: www.statravel.co.uk

Harrison Beaumont (Insurance Brokers) Ltd
tel: 01993 700200
fax: 01993 100510
website: www.hbinsurance.co.uk

Snowcard Insurance Services Limited
Lower Boddington, Daventry, Northants NN11 6XZ
tel: 01327 262805
fax: 01327 263227
website: www.snowcard.co.uk

Maps
The LK maps you will need are available from the following specialist
outlets.

Cordee Ltd
3a de Montfort Street, Leicester LE1 7HD
tel: 0116 254 3579
email: sales@cordee.co.uk
website: www.cordee.co.uk

Stanfords
12–14 Long Acre, London WC2E 9LP
tel: 020 7836 1321
email: sales@stanfords.co.uk
website: www.stanfords.co.uk

Chartech International Ltd
Parson's Lane, Hope, Hope Valley, Derbyshire S33 6RB
tel: 01433 621779
email: info@aqua3.com
website: www.aqua3.com

Travel Information

Route Summary

Even a cursory glance at the maps covering this tour shows that there is an enormous number of possible alternative routes. It would not be sensible to write a description of every combination and I have tried to strike a balance between detailed descriptions and simple suggestions of alternatives. To prevent the larger picture of the tour getting lost in the detail of the individual daily stages it is helpful to summarise it in four parts.

1. Villars to the Col du Sanetsch area
2. Sanetsch to Iffigenalp
3. Iffigenalp to Leukerbad
4. Leukerbad to Kandersteg

Map Key
Walking route
Mountaineering alternatives

Villars to the Col du Sanetsch area

I chose Villars as the starting point because of its plentiful accommodation and other facilities but it is equally feasible to base oneself in any of the villages between Bex and Villars or the hamlets east of Bex.Whilst it is possible to start on foot from Villars, most people will take advantage of the transport available to reach the interesting mountain scenery more quickly. A tramway runs between Villars and Bex, stopping at La Barboleusaz, and there is a postbus service between Bex and Les Plans.

All routes pass through the hamlet of Derborence. This is an attractive place for an overnight stop, at the inn in the hamlet itself, or at nearby Godey. The routes from La Barboleusaz and Les Plans are an easy introduction to walking in the Alps but the passage via the Cabane Rambert, given in the mountaineering alternative, is rugged and very testing for the first day out. It is, nonetheless, highly recommended to experienced, fit, Alpine walkers.

From Derborence it is a fine day's expedition to the Col du Sanetsch. This involves the ascent of the Poteu des Etales which might appear a little intimidating but has been recently improved with well-placed

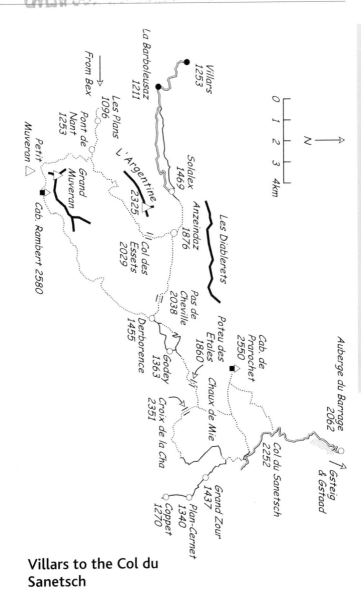

Villars to the Col du Sanetsch

metal hand holds and rope hand rails as well as two very solid ladders at the top. There is no longer a hotel at the Col du Sanetsch but there is a good inn at the nearby Barrage du Lac de Sénin (dam) as well as a very pleasant hut – the Cabane de Prarochet. A little off the line of the tour, there is more accommodation south of the col. These inns can be reached easily from the Col du Sanetsch or by a more difficult route across the Croix de la Cha.

Col du Sanetsch to Iffigenalp

In 1999 the path between the Col du Sanetsch and the Cabane des Audannes, along the Arête de l'Arpille and across the Col des Audannes, was improved and waymarked, so establishing the circular Tour de Wildhorn which is becoming increasingly popular. Our way follows part of this tour, walkers going clockwise, north of the Wildhorn, mountaineers going anticlockwise to the south. Accommodation at Iffigenalp is limited but there is a bus service to Lenk from where the tour can be continued by taking another bus, to Simmenfälle, to get back into the mountains.

The northern part of the Tour de Wildhorn is the easiest way from the Col du Sanetsch to Iffigenalp. There are good places for overnight stops at Gsteig, Gstaad, Lauenen and two SAC huts. A cable-car descends from the Barrage du lac de Sénin to Gsteig from where a frequent postbus service runs to Gstaad with connections to Lauenen and Lauenensee. The passage is nicely made by splitting it at the Gelten Hut, which can be reached from the Auberge du Barrage, or Gsteig, in 6 hours.

It is rather too much to go from the Cabane de Prarochet directly to the Gelten Hut (8¼ hours) and it would be better go to the Auberge du Sanetsch and take transport to Lauenensee from where the Gelten Hut is reached in just over 2 hours or Iffigenalp in 4¾ hours. Or, in a more relaxed fashion, descend on foot to Gsteig for the night; then go to the Gelten Hut. Starting from the inns south of the Col du Sanetsch the best option is a postbus to the dam.

It only adds an hour or so to make a detour to the Wildhorn Hut for lunch and, for those who prefer huts to inns, it makes a good overnight stop en route to the Wildstrubel Hut across the Schnidejoch.

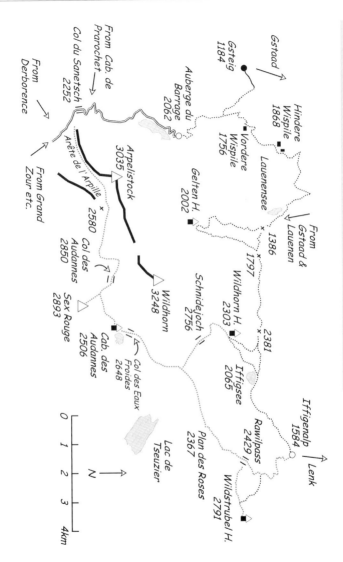

Col du Sanetsch to Iffigenalp

The mountaineering route south of the Wildhorn across the Col des Audannes, the Col des Eaux Froides and the Rawilpass is more in tune with the mountains than the northern route and not too difficult. The only accommodation en route is the Cabane des Audannes and, as this hut gets very busy in the season, especially Saturday night, it should be booked in advance. Just before reaching the Cabane des Audannes there is an easy ascent of the Sex Rouge which is a fine viewpoint. As well as the inn at Iffigenalp there is the Wildstrubel Hut which is easily reached from the Cabane des Audannes and is a good starting point for the next part of the tour.

Iffigenalp to Leukerbad

The most direct route from Iffigenalp to Leukerbad passes north of the Wildstrubel massif across the Ammertenpass to Engstligenalp, from where it crosses the Chindbettipass and descends the Rote Chumme to the Daubensee. Leukerbad is reached by a spectacular descent from the Gemmipass.

If this is your first Alpine walking holiday you should by now have a good idea of your capabilities, and if you feel up to it, you should seriously consider crossing the Ammertenpass. The last few hundred metres of this pass are somewhat rough and after bad weather they could be testing; for this reason the description of its passage is to be found in the mountaineering section of this guide. In poor conditions, or if you are disinclined to take on a rough ascent, there is a lower and easier way to Engstligenalp on less mountainous paths. In the early part of the last century this passage was made by a crossing east of the Regenboldshorn to Unter dem Birg. This way has since fallen out of use and nowadays a small col west of the Regenboldshorn, the Pommernpass, is used. This route can be started on foot from Iffigenalp, but from Lenk it is best to take a bus to the Simmenfälle. A cable-car runs between Unter dem Birg and Engstligenalp or the spectacular ascent can be made on foot in about 2 hours.

From Engstligenalp there is only a modest amount of height to gain, crossing the Chindbettipass and Rote Chumme to the Daubensee. From here it is an easy walk to Kandersteg, with refreshments and accommodation at the Berghaus Schwarenbach, but the main route continues by descending from the Gemmipass to Leukerbad. This is a

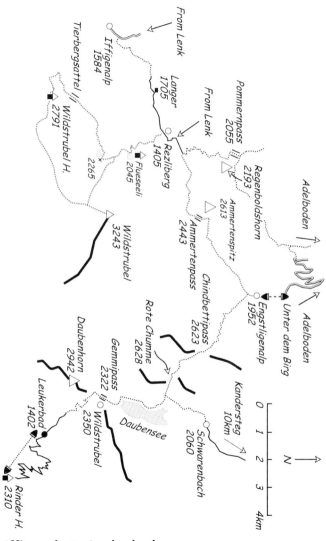

Iffigenalp to Leukerbad

pleasant resort for a day off, with the option of going to the Rinder Hut by cable-car to climb the Torrenthorn or enjoying a stroll towards the Ferdenpass.

Starting from the Wildstrubel Hut, Engstligenalp is reached in about $8^1/_4$ hours by crossing the Tierbergsattel, descending to Rezliberg and crossing the Ammertenpass. Or, in the course of two days, the Wildstrubel can be climbed and, after a night in the Flueseeli Hut or the Gasthaus Rezliberg, the walk can be continued to Engstligenalp across the Ammertenpass. If you do not want to stay in a hotel in Leukerbad there is accommodation at the Rinder Hut which is reached from the village by cable-car.

Leukerbad to Kandersteg

Kandersteg can be reached from Leukerbad in a day by taking the cable-car back to the Gemmipass and following the easy track past the Daubensee and the Berghaus Schwarenbach to Sunnbüel and either walking down or taking the cable-car to Eggeschwand. But it would be a shame to do this as the route across the Restipass to the Lötschental and the passage of the Lötschenpass to the Gasterntal is absolutely delightful. The descent from the Lötschenpass has a short glacier crossing but the glacier is dry, ie not snow covered, and almost entirely covered with debris. A marked trail has been constructed across it that avoids any crevasses and the passage does not present any problems to even modest walkers.

An overnight stop at the simple, but delightful, inn at Kummenalp is highly recommended but those preferring more luxurious accommodation can descend to the Lötschental where there are several hotels. The descent can be made by an easy traverse from Kummenalp to the Lauchernalp cable-car – where there is an inn and a hotel – or on foot all the way down.

The final part of the tour, from Kummenalp or the Lötschental, across the Lötschenpass to the Gasterntal and Kandersteg, is easily done in a single day. But if the night is passed in the Lötschental Hut, the Hockenhorn can be climbed in the early morning before descending to Kandersteg

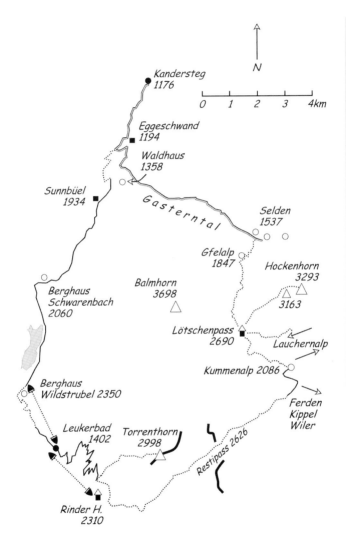

Leukerbad to Kandersteg

Part One
The Walkers' Route

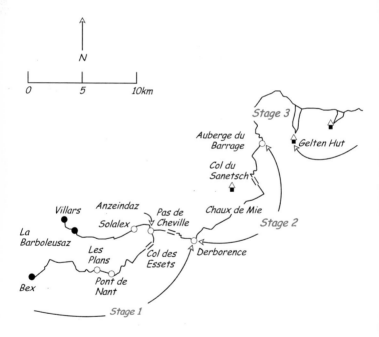

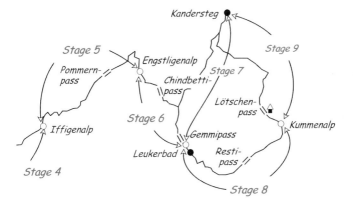

Stage 1 – Villars to Derborence

Two alternative routes are given here, the first starting from Les Plans and a second, even easier way, starting from La Barboleusaz.

Les Plans to Derborence via the Col des Essets

Distance	15km
Ascent	1,121m
Descent	736m
Time	6¼ hours

Get off the bus from Bex to Les Plans at the Restaurant l'Argentine (1,070m) and take the road along the south bank of the river for about 500m where, just past a left turn, spot height 1,087m, a track forks off left and follows the river through woods. Continue along this for 1km until a series of ladders leads up to the road where a path descends left, crosses the river then a side stream before rejoining the road at Pont de Nant (1,253m, 45 minutes). Refreshments and accommodation can be found at Auberge Communale.

From Pont de Nant follow a rough track to La Glaciére (1,374m) where a signpost indicates a jeep track to Le Richard. Just 20m beyond this a more pleasant path, waymarked with yellow as well as red and white flashes, leads off right through woods to Le Richard (1,535m, 1½ hours). Now follow a jeep track, using shortcuts across the hairpins to

La Vare (refreshments, 1,756m, 2½ hours). Do not be tempted to take the path to La Vare signposted to the Cabane de Plan Névé; it is quicker but steep and unpleasant. From La Vare, after skirting round a marshy patch, a most attractive path, marked by red and white flashes, leads north-east along the bottom of a wide valley, Plan des Bouis, with towering mountains on both sides. At the end of the plain, close to spot height 1,854m, the path steepens and works through some interesting little rock bands before easing off just before reaching the Col des Essets (2,029m, 3¾ hours). This is a

Argentine – Haute Corde (2,325m)

The ascent of the east ridge from the Col des Essets takes 1 hour and is barely more than a walk, although in a few places you may have to use your hands. There is a vertiginous view from the summit across the north face of the Argentine – a popular climbing area with many technical routes. In descent take the path from spot height 2,139m via Col de la Poreyrette (2,044m), past the Cabane Barraud to Anzeindaz. Up and down adds less than two hours to the time.

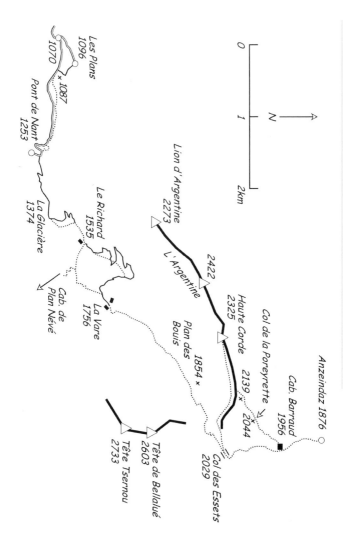

Col des Essets and the Haute Corde

splendid place for lunch, with fine views of the Dents-du-Midi and an easy climb to the summit of the Haute Corde.

The direct descent from the Col des Essets to Anzeindaz is easy; go north past the Cabane Barraud (privately owned, no accommodation, 1,956m, 4 hours) to Anzeindaz where there are two excellent inns for lunch or an overnight stop (1,876m, 4¼ hours).

From Anzeindaz go east and, almost immediately, cross a dry stream bed, which is followed at an easy gradient on an obvious, although not perfectly marked, path to Pas de Cheville (2,038m, 5 hours). Beyond the col the path continues in the same direction, past spot height 2,001m, for around 500m before turning south and working its way down a rock band. The descent becomes quite steep on scree for a short distance, crosses a stream, then eases where it passes left of a building, Le Grenier (1,744m, 5½ hours). Going east once more the path crosses another stream and descends gently through trees. Just beyond the building at Les Penés (1,660m, 5¾ hours) a left fork is signposted to Godey; you may take this if you are staying at the Auberge du Godet but it takes no longer to continue the descent through the delightful larch wood to Derborence (1,455m, 6¼ hours). Godey is reached in 45 minutes by following the road to

spot height 1,357m and taking the left fork to the hamlet (1,363m).

La Barboleusaz to Derborence

Distance	13km
Ascent	854m
Descent	610m
Time	5 hours

From the square in La Barboleusaz follow the road past the gondola station to where a signposted track, about 1km from La Barboleusaz, leads off left but almost immediately turns right. Continue along the marked path until it reaches a road at Les Ernets (1,380m, 45 minutes). Turn right and follow the road for around 100m before taking a left fork which leads to a junction with a path at spot height 1,471m (1¼ hours). Take the path through woods and cross a stream at spot height 1,472m; on the other side a track ascends gently to a rise just above Solalex. Go down the hillside to the hamlet itself (1,469m, 1¾ hours). All this can also be done by bus.

From Solalex a good track leads north-east for roughly 500m where a path forks right. Follow this with no difficulty to Anzeindaz (1,876m, 3 hours). Then follow the route described above across the Pas de Cheville to Derborence (1,455m, 5 hours).

La Barboleusaz and Anzeindaz to Derborence

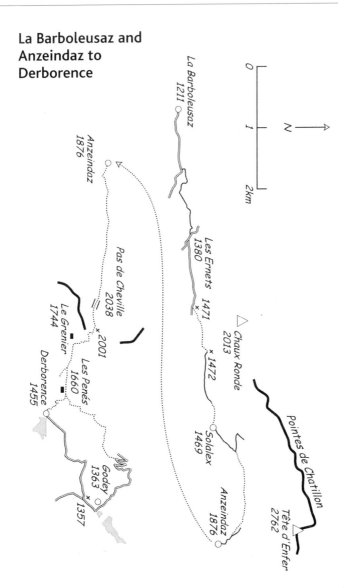

Stage 2 – Derborence to the Auberge du Barrage (Col du Sanetsch)

Distance	18km
Ascent	1,108m
Descent	501m
Time	7¼ hours

Derborence to the Chaux de Mie

This makes an interesting day with an entertaining, but easy, scramble at the Poteu des Etales* followed by good ground to the Col du Sanetsch. There is accommodation at the Auberge du Barrage or Gsteig, which is easily reached by cable-car. Alternatively, the night can be passed at the Cabane de Prarochet. There is also some accommodation south of the Col.

At the Refuge du Lac a signpost indicates a route to Sanetsch, but this path gains unnecessary height and it is better to go down the road for about 500m where a path is signed to La Tour. Follow this across the Eboulement des Diablerets – the remains of two great stonefalls in 1714 and 1719 – as far as the road between Godey and La Tour, descend two hairpins, cross a river and contour to the hamlet of La Lui (45 minutes).

Starting from Godey take the road to the dam where a track and a path (not exactly as shown on LK) lead to the road at La Lui. Go north-east on the road but, almost immediately, fork right on a path that makes a little height, in woodland, before reaching a bridge across the river, La Lizerne (1,584m, 1¼ hours). Do not cross the bridge but take a left fork and ascend ground which gradually becomes steeper until it reaches the bottom of the Poteu des Etales (1,860m, 2¾ hours).

The cliff ahead is split by a vertical gash about 80m high. Start by scrambling up large, stable blocks with metal handholds, then tackle more broken and steeper ground, which is protected by fixed ropes. Just below the top, two well-constructed ladders lead to a final fixed rope. Then it's easier ground, where a pleasant path leads east to chalets at 2,094m (3½ hours). Continue eastwards, descending slightly through a narrow, rocky defile to an open plain before ascending a little to a junction, with a signpost. The right fork leads to Croix de la Cha, a difficult mountaineering alternative.

This strange name is thought to be a double corruption of Porteur de Bois. Before the Croix de la Cha was established, wood for the lime burners around the Alpe de Mie was carried by porters across the Porteur de Bois. The name became Poteu des Etales from the dialect words for log: étalle or ételle.

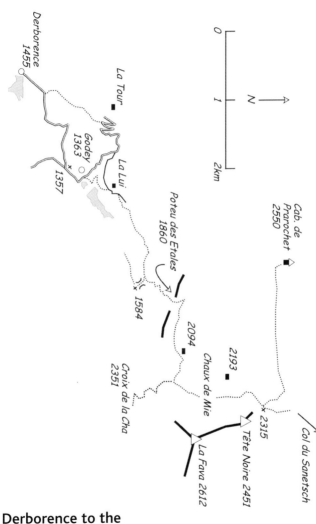

**Derborence to the
Chaux de Mie and the
Cabane de Prarochet**

Turn left (north) on an obvious path, which crosses Chaux de Mie, beneath the west face of La Fava and passes an isolated building (2,193m, 4 hours) to reach a small col (not named on LK) at spot height 2,315m (4½ hours).

The path divides at the col; the left fork goes to the Cabane de Prarochet; straight on for the Auberge du Barrage.

Chaux de Mie to the Auberge du Barrage

For the Auberge du Barrage continue north-east, then north, to the west of the small lakes of Sex Rouge, before turning north-east again at a junction by spot height 2,303m – snow plaques are possible here even late in the season – to reach the head of the pretty valley of Les Cloujons. A well-marked passage leading between sheets of limestone crosses Plan de la Fontaine to reach the chalets of Tsanfleuron (2,114m, 5½ hours). A track parallel to the road leads directly to the Col du Sanetsch (2,252m, 6 hours). Beyond

the col a couple of hairpins on the road can be avoided by a path, then follow the road for around 300m until another path turns off right towards the east bank of the Lac de Sénin. An excellent path runs along the east bank of the lake and rejoins the road just below the Auberge du Barrage (2,062m, 7¼ hours). Accommodation here and a small *folklorique* museum as well.

This is a pleasant place to spend the night and leaves you well positioned for the next stage of the tour. If the Auberge is full, there are two hotels in Gsteig, which is easily reached by cable-car (last descent 17:00). From Gsteig there is a regular postbus service to Gstaad and Lauenen, where there is yet more accommodation.

Rooms are also available in the inns to the south of the Col du Sanetsch although they are off the line of the tour. They are served by a postbus that leaves the former Hotel du Sanetsch at 17:06. A useful morning bus reaches the col at 10:43 and the barrage (dam) at 11:03 (see

Cabane de Prarochet
This hut is easily reached in 1¼ hours from the col at spot height 2,315m; see the previous sketch map on p35. The left fork to the Cabane de Prarochet is not shown on LK but the route to the hut is well marked. Follow the paint flashes and marker poles across a fascinating moonscape of limestone and enjoy the magnificent views of the Pennine Alps to the south before reaching the Cabane de Prarochet (2,550m), 5¾ hours from Derborence.

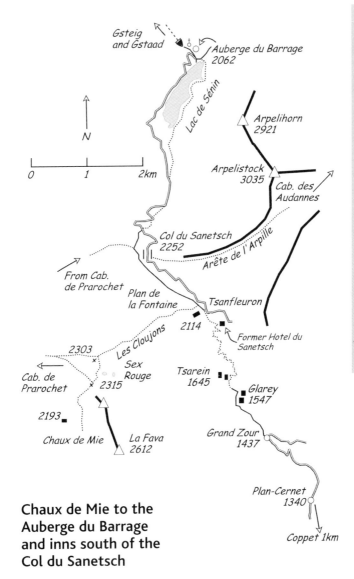

Gsteig and Gstaad

Auberge du Barrage
2062

Lac de Sénin

Arpelihorn
2921

Arpelistock
3035

Cab. des
Audannes

N

0   1   2km

Col du Sanetsch
2252

Arête de l'Arpille

From Cab.
de Prarochet

Plan de
la Fontaine

Tsanfleuron

Les Cloujons   2114

Former Hotel du
Sanetsch

2303

Sex
Rouge

Tsarein
1645

Cab. de
Prarochet   2315

Glarey
1547

2193

Chaux de Mie   La Fava
2612

Grand Zour
1437

Plan-Cernet
1340

Coppet 1km

**Chaux de Mie to the
Auberge du Barrage
and inns south of the
Col du Sanetsch**

Appendix C for more information). This leaves plenty of time to do the next stage of the walk. On foot descend a steep path with many zig-zags from Tsanfleuron (2,114m) to Tsarein (1,645m, 6¼ hours) then a track to the Auberge du Tsanfleuron at Grand Zour (1,437m, 6¾ hours). Continuing down the road, the Auberge du Plan-Cernet (1,340m) is reached in 7¼ hours, and the Auberge Beau Site at Coppet (1,270m) in 7½ hours.

Stage 3 – Auberge du Barrage to the Gelten Hut

Distance	15km
Ascent	1,006m
Descent	1,066m
Time	6 hours

From the Auberge du Barrage follow a rough road north-east for about 150m to a junction signed 'Bergwanderweg'. Take the left fork and, after a further 150m, fork right (north), ignoring a faint path to the left, and lose a little height to spot height 2,002m. Descend in zig-zags, steep at first, until easy ground is reached east of the Sanetschfall. All this is quite delightful, well graded and in magnificent rock scenery. At Rotengraben (1,478m, 1 hour) cross a bridge and fork right to pass above chalets at Burg (1,511m, 1¼ hours). Keep right on a metalled track, cross two streams before turning a hairpin at spot height 1,607m and continuing up zig-zags to Vordere Wispile (1,748m, 2 hours). LK shows two paths to Hindere Wispile but the northernmost is rather boggy and ill-defined in places and the natural way is to follow the farm track past the viewpoint (1,983m) to Hindere Wispile (1,866m, 2¾ hours). Take the path signed to the Krinnenpass but at spot height 1,752m turn sharp right. After about 1km cross a track then, around 200m further on, turn right on the same track. Make a traversing descent south of the Lauenensee to a bridge at spot height 1,386m (3¾ hours).

For the Gelten Hut, cross the bridge and turn right on a well-marked path that ascends, steeply in places, through trees above the torrent of the Geltenbach. Just before spot height 1,604m the path splits, but the right-hand way has fallen into disrepair so go left and enter a beautiful cwm (4½ hours). This is a good place to stop for lunch and admire the Geltenschuss in the distance. Cross the Geltenbach and follow the stream for about 600m before turning right where the path becomes steep again as it makes its way above the top of the waterfall.

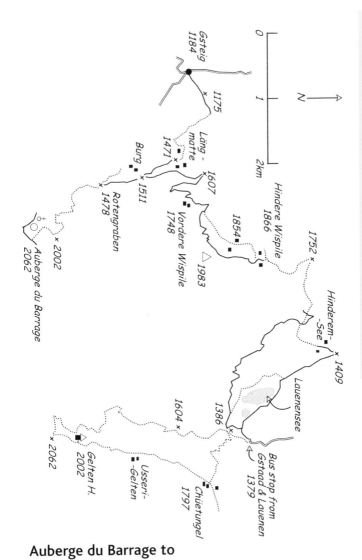

Stage 3 – Auberge du Barrage to the Gelten Hut

Auberge du Barrage to the Gelten Hut

Descend slightly and cross another bridge before a final, easy ascent to the Gelten Hut (2,002m, 6 hours).

One level up from the hut there is an attractive little circular tour of the Rottal plateau on obvious paths crossing a stream close to spot height 2,062m where there are tremendous views of waterfalls coming from the remnants of the Gelten glacier high above.

Stage 3a – Cabane de Prarochet and Gsteig to the Gelten Hut

Having passed the night at the Cabane de Prarochet it is too far to get to the Gelten Hut on foot in a single day. The alternatives are to take transport from the Auberge du Barrage to Lauenensee and walk from there or to pass a night in Gsteig.

Cabane de Prarochet to Gsteig

Distance	15km
Ascent	64m
Descent	1,430m
Time	3¾ hours

From the Cabane de Prarochet follow a waymarked path that passes close to spot height 2,507m before descending to the moraine at spot height 2,381m where there is an interesting view of the snout of the Tsanfleuron glacier. Continue walking north-east, keeping right at all the forks, to reach the Col du Sanetsch (1 hour). Follow the description in the previous Stage 3 to the Auberge du Barrage (2,062m, 2 hours) and descend past the Sanetschfall to Rotengraben (1,478m, 2 hours). Cross the bridge and turn immediately left (the right turn leads to Burg) on a good path through a wood. Pass under the cableway near the bottom station of the cable-car to join a road which leads directly to Gsteig (1,184m, 3¾ hours).

A Relaxing Day

For a really easy day take a postbus from Gsteig to Gstaad, have a coffee (surprisingly affordable) and look at the clothes (shockingly expensive) in the shop windows whilst waiting for the bus to take you on to Lauenensee. It is a brief 5 minutes walk from the bus stop at Lauenensee to the bridge at spot height 1,386m, and then another 2 hours to reach the hut. Or you can even go directly to Iffigenalp – see Stage 4.

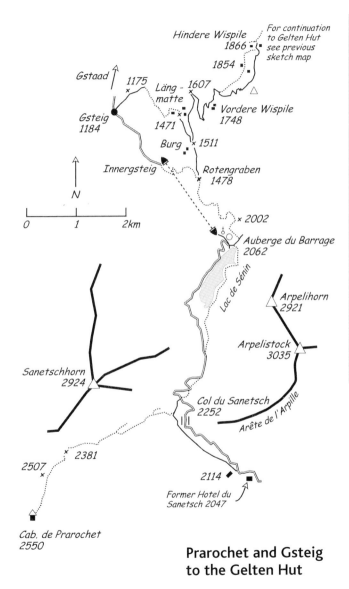

For continuation
to Gelten Hut
see previous
sketch map

Hindere Wispile
1866

1854

Gstaad 1175

Läng-
matte 1607

Gsteig
1184

1471

Vordere Wispile
1748

Burg 1511

Innergsteig

Rotengraben
1478

N

0   1   2km

× 2002

Auberge du Barrage
2062

Lac de Sénin

Arpelihorn
2921

Arpelistock
3035

Sanetschhorn
2924

Col du Sanetsch
2252

Arête de l'Arpille

× 2381

2507

2114

Former Hotel du
Sanetsch 2047

Cab. de Prarochet
2550

**Prarochet and Gsteig
to the Gelten Hut**

Gsteig to the Gelten Hut

Distance	15km
Ascent	1,300m
Descent	482m
Time	6 hours

Go north-east on a track opposite the Hotel Bären, cross a river at spot height 1,175m and after 300m turn right. Ascend easily through Längmatte (1,471m, 1 hour) to Burg (1,511m, 1¼ hours) and follow the route described in Stage 3 through Vordere Wispile and Hindere Wispile, to the bridge at spot height 1,386m (3¾ hours). Continue alongside the Geltenbach to the Gelten Hut (2,002m, 6 hours).

Stage 4 – Gelten Hut to Iffigenalp

Distance	11km
Ascent	644m
Descent	1,062m
Time	4 hours

The path from the hut (signposted) makes a little height to start before descending across steep ground protected by chains (hardly necessary) until, finally, a ladder leads to open pastures at Chüetungel (1,797m, 45 minutes). Pass between the farm buildings to a junction where the signpost to Iffigenalp is marked 'Vorsicht' – care. In fact, this way goes quite easily, although the descent in bad weather could be trying. So, take the right fork, make height over stony ground and cross a scree slope where the path works under a cliff. Now, with a little exposure, gain a small bluff, where a few stiff upward passages lead to good zig-zags and a final, easy, approach to spot height 2,271m (2¼ hours). Go on to spot height 2,381m (2½ hours). There are fine views and it's a good spot for lunch.

Descend towards Iffigsee then gain a little height beyond the lake to spot height 2,086m (3 hours). A fork is shown on LK but only the northern-most path is obvious on the ground;

Wildhorn Hut

The Wildhorn Hut is reached by a path that breaks away right, just beyond spot height 2,381m and turns the north-east ridge of the Niesehorn. When the hut comes in sight descend to a moraine trough before ascending roughish ground to the hut (2,303m, 1 hour). To descend to Iffigenalp, return to the moraine trough and follow a path north-east along its base. Keep high above Iffigsee to spot height 2,086m (30 minutes), and descend through Groppi to Iffigenalp (1,584m, 1½ hours).

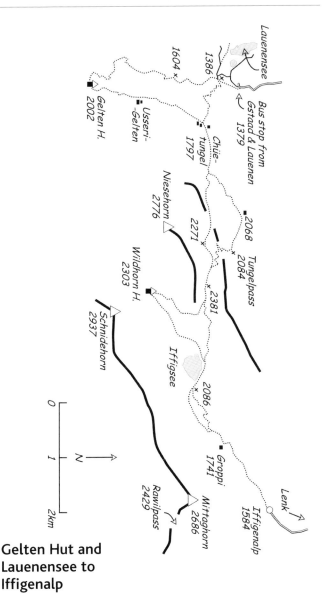

Gelten Hut and Lauenensee to Iffigenalp

follow this to Groppi (1,741m, 3½ hours), from where it is a pleasant descent alongside the Iffigbach to Iffigenalp (1,584m, 4 hours).

Alternatively, at the Vorsicht sign, take the left fork to a farm at 2,068m and go to the Tungelpass (2,084m, 1¾ hours). From the pass, a steep but well-made path crosses a rock band to join the direct path east of spot height 2,271m and so to spot height 2,381m (2¾ hours).

Continue to Iffigenalp as above (4¼ hours). You can find accommodation here or take the bus to Lenk.

Lauenensee to Iffigenalp

From the bus stop go south on the path signed 'Kuetungel' (Chüetungel) for 400m then turn north-west and zig-zag steeply up through woods to Chüetungel (1½ hours). Continue as above to Iffigenalp (4¾ hours).

Stage 5 – Iffigenalp to Engstligenalp

From Iffigenalp

Distance	20km
Ascent	1,152m
Descent	1,336m
Time	7½ hours

From Simmenfälle

Distance	15km
Ascent	1,114m
Descent	819m
Time	6¼ hours

The best way of getting to Engstligenalp from Iffigenalp is across the Ammertenpass but, as already noted, this way is fairly rugged on the south side and after a spell of bad weather can be difficult. For this reason, the description of this passage is included as a mountaineering alternative, but in good conditions strong walkers should have no problems with it. The way described here is just as long but is very easy underfoot.

If the night were passed in Lenk the best approach is to take a bus to the Simmenfälle and start from there. This way is shorter than that from Iffigenalp and passes by a magnificent waterfall.

Iffigenalp to the Pommernpass

From the inn at Iffigenalp go north-east on the road for about 600m, where a path turns off right, crosses a river, and ascends through Ritz and Langermatte before descending to Langer (1,705m, 1½ hours). Continue eastwards past the inn at Rezliberg (1,405m) to a bridge (1,379m,

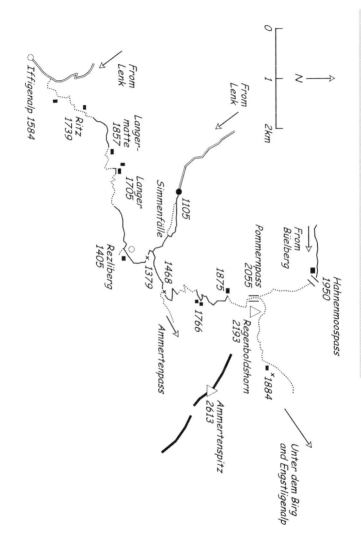

Iffigenalp to the Pommernpass

2¼ hours). Cross the river and, after about 150m, take a right fork on a farm track to a further junction at spot height 1,468m (2½ hours).

Starting from Lenk take a bus to the roadhead at 1,105m. A beautiful path follows the stream to the Simmenfälle, where a walkway crosses the cataract. A track continues through woods to a junction on the path from Iffigenalp, 150m before the bridge at 1,379m (45 minutes). Fork left to the junction at spot height 1,468m (1 hour).

Go straight ahead (the right fork goes to Ammertenpass) crossing and recrossing a river. Ascend two steep zig-zags before leaving the track on a path through woods. Continue past chalets at 1,766m (Pommernalp, 3½ hours), and 1,875m where a path leads to the pass (2,055m, 4½ hours). From the Simmenfälle this is more like 3¼ hours.

Pommernpass to Engstligenalp

From the pass a good path contours round the Regenboldshorn turning gently to the east before rising slightly as it passes beneath a cableway to reach a grassy saddle. Ignore a right fork and descend to a junction by a barn, (2,042m). It makes little difference which way you go here but the path to the right is possibly better. Go easily down

> ### A Shortcut to Adelboden
> Where the track divides near spot height 1,828m take the left fork and descend gently to reach a road at spot height 1,594m (5¼ hours). Cross the road and continue in much the same direction on a path which soon joins another road. Go left to the gondola station at Berglager (1,486m, 6 hours) and make the interesting descent by gondola.

towards the bottom of the valley, keeping right at a building near spot height 1,884m. A good track leads across the valley floor over a marshy area, Bütschi, to a further fork near spot height 1,828m (5¼ hour).

Take the right fork and ascend across a hillside to reach the Troneggrat where, about 300m past spot height 1,966m, a path leads to a metalled road that descends via several hairpins to Unter dem Birg (1,400m, 7½ hours); from the Simmenfälle about 6 hours. You can take the cable-car to Engstligenalp from here but, if you started from the Simmenfälle, you may have the energy to make the ascent on foot. For Adelboden, continue along the Troneggrat and pick up the road north of Chuenisbärgli (1,738m, 6 hours). Go down the road using paths to cut corners to spot height 1,326m (7 hours) where a track leads across the river into Adelboden (1,348m, 7½ hours).

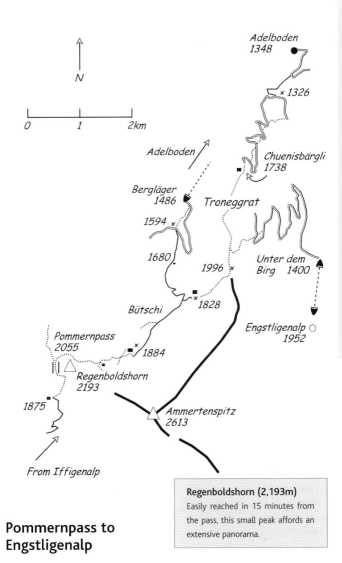

↑
N

0   1   2km

Adelboden
1348 ●

× 1326

Adelboden ↗

Chuenisbärgli
1738 ■

Bergläger
1486

Troneggrat

1594 ×

1680 ■

1996 ×

Unter dem
Birg 1400

Bütschi

1828 ×
■

Engstligenalp ○
1952

Pommernpass
2055

△

× 1884
■

Regenboldshorn
2193

1875 ■

△ *Ammertenspitz*
2613

From Iffigenalp ↗

Regenboldshorn (2,193m)
Easily reached in 15 minutes from
the pass, this small peak affords an
extensive panorama.

Pommernpass to
Engstligenalp

Stage 6 – Engstligenalp to Leukerbad

Distance	14km
Ascent	906m
Descent	1,456m
Time	6 hours

From the inns follow a track south-west, turn left just before the second bridge, spot height 1,937m (signposted) and go south-east to the leftmost of the Märbenen barns (1,963m, 15 minutes). Make height up grass and rocks, it's waymarked but there are many false paths to start with, until a small lake is reached by spot height 2,350m (1 hour). Continue in the same direction up steep, but stable, scree to the Chindbettipass (2,623m, 2 hours).

A traversing descent on scree leads to moraine below the Tälli Glacier, around 2,510m. Cross two streams with care and pull up to the ridge ahead, close to spot height 2,628m (2³⁄₄ hours). Go down through rockbands towards the Daubensee. There are steep zig-zags at first, but the gradient soon moderates. The path passes between red outcrops at the head of Rote Chumme to a relatively flat area where a path goes left to the Berghaus Schwarenbach; ignore this and continue down to join the path that circumnavigates the lake (3¹⁄₄ hours). Walk south to the far end of the lake where the way divides. Take the left fork and,

after about 200m, cross a bridge on a marked path to the left of a cableway before passing under it to arrive at the Gemmipass (2,322m, 4¹⁄₄ hours). It is only a matter of moments before you are refreshing yourself in the newly-built Berghaus Wildstrubel (2,350m) and enjoying the magnificent views of the Bernese and Pennine Alps. By the Berghaus is a cable-car that goes directly down to Leukerbad but the descent on foot is excellent and not to be missed.

This remarkable passage is documented with great glee in the 19th-century editions of Baedeker's guide to Switzerland: 'The windings are skilfully hewn in the rock, often resembling a spiral staircase, the upper parts actually projecting in places beyond the lower. The steepest parts and most sudden corners are protected by parapets'. I can give no better description than this. From the Berghaus Wildstrubel descend south-west past the old hotel to a junction where the left turning goes over the brink of the 500m rock wall and descends exactly as described by Baedeker. The bottom of the steep rock is reached at spot height 1,679m (5¹⁄₄ hours) then the way is less vertiginous, passing a junction at spot height 1,539m (5¹⁄₂ hours), and proceeding easily to Leukerbad (1,402m, 6 hours).

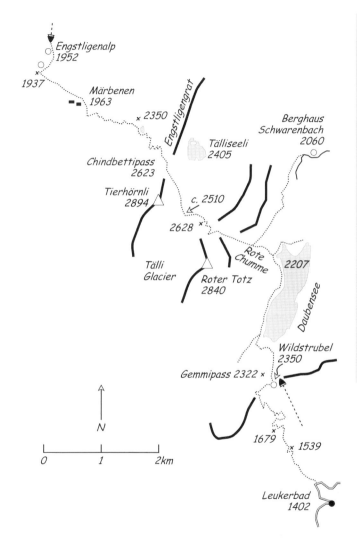

Engstligenalp to Leukerbad

Stage 7 – Leukerbad to Kandersteg via the Gemmipass

Distance	16km
Ascent	50m
Descent	1,224m
Time	3¾ hours

This is a quick way to get to Kandersteg from Leukerbad if time is short. Although the descent from the Gemmipass is fascinating, most people going this way will use the cable-car to reach it from Leukerbad. The timings above assume this; going all the way on foot it will take approximately 7½ hours. This is certainly the easiest way to get to Kandersteg but it is not very interesting and the routes described in stages 8 and 9 are much better.

From the cable-car station (2,350m) take the track which descends gently towards the east bank of the Daubensee and follow it to the northern end of the lake, where it descends a little more steeply before contouring to the Berghaus Schwarenbach (2,060m, 1 hour). Another descent leads to a relatively flat alp. Passing between a building and a long, low wall by a river the path reaches a small bridge at 1,872m (1½ hours).

At this point the path divides. The left fork goes to the cable-car station at Sunnbüel in about 20 minutes, from where a regular service runs to Eggeschwand. To continue on foot take the right fork which, after passing the bottom of a ski-lift, enters an attractive wooded area where many of the flowers and shrubs have name labels. At Stock (1,834m, 2 hours) a path descends, steeply in places, to join a road just south of the bottom station of the cable-car (3 hours). There is a bus service from the cable-car station to Kandersteg and if you are lucky you will catch the one driven by a charming lady who, as well as speaking perfect English, more or less runs a taxi service to visitors' hotels in bad weather.

To walk to Kandersteg take a path across the river before reaching the cable-car station and follow it past the International Scout Centre until it reaches a road at spot height 1,181m. Continue on the road passing under the railway and over a river to join the main road which leads directly to Kandersteg (1,176m, 3¾ hours).

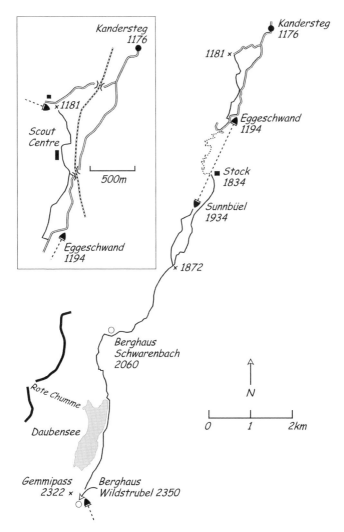

**Gemmipass to
Kandersteg**

Stage 8 – Leukerbad to Kummenalp

Distance	12km
Ascent	373m
Descent	597m
Time	3½ hours

There is little merit in walking the track from Leukerbad to the Rinder Hut; take the cable-car or add 3¾ hours to the times given here. At the hut a phalanx of paths leads south and south-east; keeping always to the highest path, contour round the south-west spur of the Torrenthorn to spot height 2,397m (45 minutes). Continue contouring as the path turns north-east, then descend slightly to the Wysse See (1 hour). In about 700m the path starts to climb and without difficulty reaches the Restipass (2,626m, 2¼ hours). There are fine views from here, especially of the Bietschhorn.

Just below the col there is usually a small snowfield, even at the end of the season, but this presents no problems and beyond it the way is well marked with red and white flashes. Rock and scree soon give way to grassy moraine and a pleasant path leads to Restialp (2,098m, 3 hours); you'll find refreshments and good views of part of the Pennine Alps. A high level path leads to a simple but attractive inn at Kummenalp (2,086m, 3½ hours).

If there is no accommodation available here, or if you prefer the comfort of a hotel, continue walking along the path through Hockenalp* (2,048m) to reach the accommodation between Stafel and Lauchernalp (4¼ hours). From Lauchernalp a cable-car descends to the valley where there is hotel accommodation. These hotels can be reached directly from Restialp by a steep descent to Ferden (1,375m, 4¼ hours) and continuing through Kippel (1,376m, 4¾ hours) to Wiler (1,419m, 5¼ hours).

Leukerbad to Kummenalp via the Torrenthorn

The ascent of the Torrenthorn from the Rinder Hut is described on page 90 (2 hours). To continue to the Restipass, descend from spot height 2,748m on a poor path to the Hotel Torrenthorn (3½ hours). Traverse east across rocky ground for 300m then descend to join the path from the Rinder Hut to the pass at spot height 2,331m (3¾ hours). From here it is 3½ hours to Kummenalp – a total time of 7¼ hours.

---

*There is some inconsistency between local names and names on the LK maps. The following nomenclature is adopted here: the top of the cable-car (Holz on LK) is Lauchernalp; the top of the next cableway (closed in summer) is Stafel (2,104m); the other Stafel (2,048m on LK) is Hockenalp.

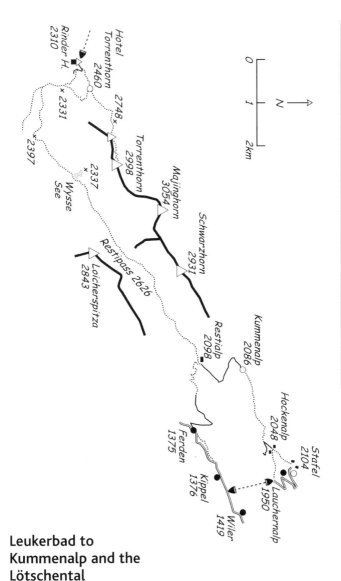

**Leukerbad to
Kummenalp and the
Lötschental**

Stage 9 – Kummenalp to Kandersteg

Distance	19km
Ascent	604m
Descent	1,514m
Time	6¾ hours

The traverse of the Lötschenpass to Kandersteg allows a wonderful contrast between the mountain atmosphere of the pass and the more gentle charm of the Gastern Valley. From Kummenalp it's no problem to go directly to Kandersteg in around 6¾ hours. However, from the Lötschental to Kandersteg is as much as 9 hours on foot and it is better to take the cable-car to Lauchernalp or split the route and stay overnight in the Lötschenpass Hut.

Go west from the inn at Kummenalp, keeping above the chalets, and turn a rocky knoll on the right where a clearly-marked path ascends easy ground. Just beyond spot height 2,415m (45 minutes), the ground becomes steeper and more rocky until, by a junction with a minor path, there is a judiciously placed metal handhold. Continue without difficulty on a well-graded path, passing spot height 2,652m (1½ hours), where the gradient eases and a plateau is reached. This is a delightful spot with impressive rock scenery and a number of tarns to work between until an area of interesting, large boulders leads to the Lötschenpass (2,690m, 2 hours).

Starting from the Lötschental take the cable-car to Lauchernalp and ascend pleasant meadows to a track at Stafel. Turn right then left past the Berghaus Lauchernalp and gain height trending westwards under a cableway. A good path makes height easily across the hillside, passing a junction where a path descends left to Hockenalp, to reach a stream crossing at spot height 2,372m (1¼ hours). On the far side of the stream a stiff pull up to Sattlegi (2,566m, 2 hours) is followed by a fine path that works across the flank of the Hockenhorn for rather more than 2km to the Lötschenpass (2,690m, 2¾ hours).

From the pass a cairned path leads across rocks and several small snow-fields, steep in places but protected by a fixed wire, until it reaches the lateral moraine of the Lötschen Glacier. Take the path along the moraine to a signpost (2½ hours) starting from Kummenalp. Ignore the old route through rocks on the right, marked with blue Bergweg signs, and take the walking trail, marked with red and white flashes, across the glacier aiming for the red and white bullseye on a prominent rock near Balme (2,403m, 2¾ hours). The glacier is almost entirely debris covered and a marked trail has been constructed across it that avoids any crevasses. At the end of the glacier

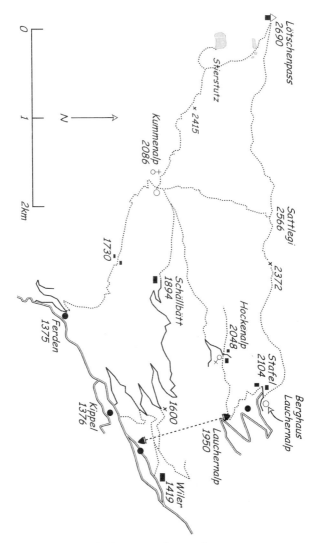

**Kummenalp and the Lötschental
to the Lötschenpass**

the path zig-zags down steep ground and turns a rocky promontory to reach Schönbüel (1,993m, 3¼ hours). Continue descending to Gfelalp (refreshments and accommodation) and pass a waterfall to a river which is crossed by an interesting suspension bridge to Selden (1,537m, 4 hours); there are refreshments and accommodation here as well. It is 11km to Kandersteg and if this seems too much there is a bus service – see Appendix C. However, walking through the lower reaches of the Gasterntal is delightful. Start by following the road until, just past Brandhubel (1,605m) a track forks off left and descends to a bridge at spot height 1,429m. Cross the river and follow a track through woods, recrossing the river at spot height 1,395m (4¾ hours). The path soon crosses the river yet again, then a tributary, before it crosses an open plain and, passing the path to the Balmhorn Hut, arrives at the Waldhaus (1,358m, 5½ hours). Go behind the inn and walk beside a stream that rejoins the main river, which is followed until it can be crossed to arrive at Eggeschwand (1,194m, 6 hours).

As already noted, there is a bus service from Eggeschwand to Kandersteg. To walk, either double back to the path which crosses the river south of the cable-car station, or take the road as far as the railway bridge and cross the river by the International Scout Centre, where a track leads to a road at spot height 1,181m. Follow a minor road under the railway and over the river to join the main road which leads directly to Kandersteg (1,176m, 6¾ hours).

The Hockenhorn

There is little difficulty in reaching the base of the Kleinhockenhorn but the Hockenhorn itself is more difficult. From the hut follow flashes north-east towards a ridge of red rock, descend a few metres then work up to the top of the ridge; it's cairned but needs a little concentration on route finding. Now it is only steep walking past spot height 2,984m (45 minutes), to the base of first peak, the Kleinhockenhorn (1¼ hours). Unfortunately, the ascent of this impressive rock tower is a graded rock climb and outside the scope of this guide. Between the lesser peak and the Hockenhorn is a snowfield which, if soft, may be passable by a walking party who then have only some easy scrambling to the summit (3,293m, 2 hours). However, the snow is often hard and, in places, icy. In these dangerous conditions it is safer to follow the cairned path that breaks away just beyond spot height 2,984m to skirt beneath the snowfield to reach the west ridge of the peak somewhat below the direct path. By this means the summit is reached in 2¼ hours. Reckon on 2¼ hours for the round trip to the Kleinhockenhorn and 3½ hours for the Hockenhorn.

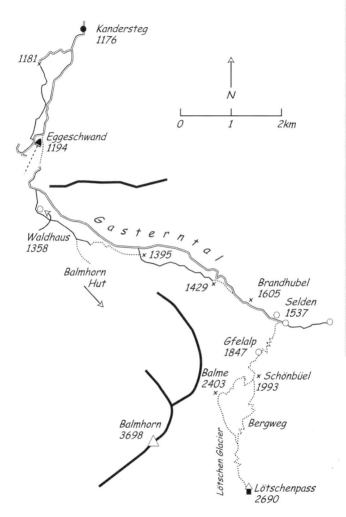

Lötschenpass to Kandersteg

Part Two
Mountaineering Alternatives

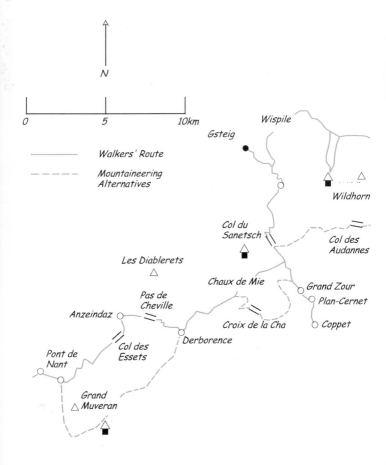

Les Plans to Derborence via the Cabane Rambert

The ascent from Pont de Nant is quite rugged and crosses some steep ground. The way from the Cabane Rambert to Derborence is part of the Tour des Muverans, it is well marked and presents no difficulties.

Les Plans to the Cabane Rambert

Distance	8km
Ascent	1,596m
Descent	84m
Time	6¼ hours

From Les Plans follow Stage 1 to Pont de Nant (1,253m, 45 minutes). Go east following the track towards Le Richard but after 300m take a right fork (south-east, old sign) and work up the hillside on a poorly marked trail for 20 minutes, until the way turns south-west. This is easy to miss and if you arrive at a dry streambed with no path ahead you have gone too far, so go back about 40m to find a faint path marked by some stones on the ground. From now on there are no problems in following the way as it winds up through trees and flowers to La Larze (1,584m, 1½ hours).

Beyond the chalet the path works up an easy slope – care is needed to spot the waymarks on grass-covered rocks – and turns a grassy crest at spot height 1,861m (2½ hours).

Cross a scree slope and pass through a notch in a ridge before working up ledges and narrow rakes across the steep couloirs of the west flank of the Pointe des Encrennes (Encrenes on LK50) and the Grand Muveran to spot height 2,199m (4 hours). This section is protected by fixed chains but could nonetheless be difficult early in the season. Now a pleasant traverse leads across the face of the mountain to a shoulder marked by an old signpost, just east of Truche du Liapay (2,297m, 4½ hours). From here it is a hard pull up to the Frête de Saille (2,584m, 5½ hours).

Just below the col are the foundations of the former Cabane Rambert. The path descends above these across a steep scree slope, not always easy to follow and a little delicate in places. In the early season there can be a number of snow plaques to cross where the path starts to regain the height lost. A short, easy, gully leads directly to the Cabane Rambert (2,582m, 6¼ hours). The view south is a stunning panorama of peaks from the Pennine Alps to Mont Blanc.

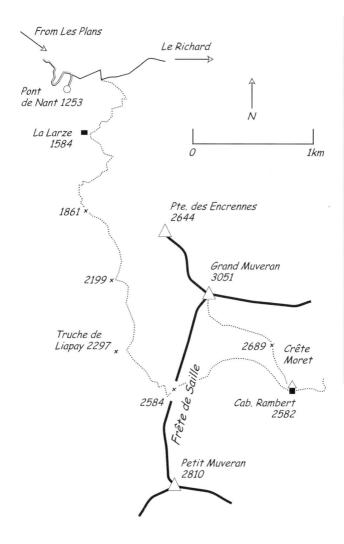

Les Plans to the Cabane Rambert

Cabane Rambert to Derborence

Distance	11km
Ascent	141m
Descent	1,268m
Time	3½ hours

This is a short and easy day and there would be plenty of time to climb the Grand Muveran before going to Derborence.

For Derborence, go east from the hut, keep right at a cairn and go over a grassy knoll before descending left over broken ground to reach an area of scree; all this is well marked. Cross the scree, it's quite stable, to reach a small rock-band at around 2,400m. Work up easily through this and follow steepish zig-zags to the Col de la Forcla (2,541m, 45 minutes). From the col go west (signposted) for about 50m to a large rock and descend to the edge of the Glacier de la Forcla. Nowadays the glacier is very shrunken and free from any significant crevasses; with care it is safe to cross. On the far side there is

an obvious red flash on a rock. Aim for this but, once on the rocks, do not ascend the line of flashes which lead to the ridge above and Le Pacheu – a graded climb that is outside the scope of this guide. Instead keep low and, making an excursion back on to the glacier, pass north of two lakes to reach a small dam at spot height 2,450m (1½ hours). Do not cross the dam but descend east, then north-east, working in and out of water-worn limestone outcrops across the Plan des Fosses to spot height 2,222m (1¾ hours). Continue north-east for 1km when the path swings left and descends the left bank of a gorge before turning further left, then right across an open hillside to La Chaux (1,956m, 2½ hours). Refreshments and simple accommodation can be found here – it's a pleasant place to stop for a drink and sample the home-made serac, a delightful and compact white cheese. To continue to Derborence descend south then south-east and cross the river Derbonne. Follow the marked path, crossing and recrossing the river until, finally, a short passage through

Grand Muveran (3,051m)

The normal route is no more than a scramble, Alpine Grade I, and is climbed from the hut by a huge disjointed zig-zag on the south face. Go up the Crête Moret and ascend north on scree (path), cross one or two rock bands taking care not to go too far to the left, where there are several false paths. Climb a large oblique chimney, flanked to the left by a yellowish tower, go up another 30m and slant left ascending on ledges (good track) to the summit (2 hours).

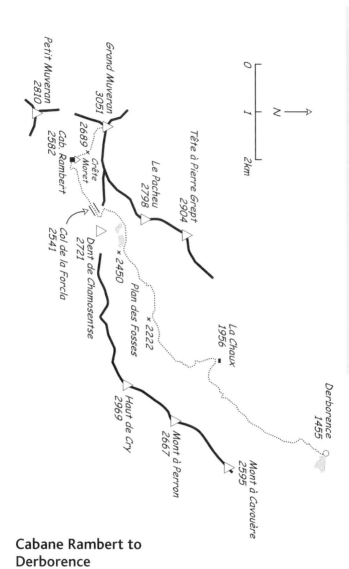

0   1   2km

N →

Petit Muveran 2810

Grand Muveran 3051

Crête 2689 × Moret

Cab. Rambert 2582

Tête à Pierre Grept 2904

Le Pacheu 2798

Col de la Forcla 2541

Dent de Chamosentse 2721

× 2450

Plan des Fosses

× 2222

La Chaux 1956

Derborence 1455

Haut de Cry 2969

Mont à Perron 2667

Mont à Cavouère 2595

Cabane Rambert to Derborence

trees leads to Derborence (1,455m, 3½ hours). For Godey, where there is also accommodation, follow the road to spot height 1,357m and take the left fork to the hamlet (1,363m, 4¼ hours). See Page 33 for a map.

Derborence to Grand Zour via the Croix de la Cha*

Distance	17km
Ascent	966m
Descent	984m
Time	6¾ hours

This is a difficult variant that tackles a steep and potentially problematic scree slope. Early in the season, or after a spell of bad weather, this section can be plastered in snow and would not be passable without an ice-axe and rope. It is for very experienced mountain walkers only. Follow Stage 2, page 34, as far as the chalets at 2,094m (3½ hours) and continue to the signposted junction. LK shows two paths leading to the Croix de la Cha. Avoid the path which makes a long dog-leg south-west to spot height 2,172m before turning to the col as it is regularly swept by scree from the steep slopes under Petit Mont Gond and is not maintained. Instead, follow the well-marked path which goes directly to the col in a series of zig-zags. Initially it is not too steep but, after crossing a stream-bed, it gains height more rapidly on a stony, grass slope. Cross a vertiginous and some-what unstable scree slope, which is often slippery, and go up several zig-zags cut into the rocks to reach Croix de la Cha (2,351m, 4½ hours). After this arduous ascent the panorama is particularly agreeable and in the early part of the season there are wild flowers in abundance. Descend to a junction just north of a small lake, Etang de Trente Pas (2,196m) keep left and work across some rough ground before a gentle descent to chalets at 1,945m (5¼ hours). A track leads north-east then north, passing through a narrow gap at the base of a spur at 1,969m descending from La Fava. Continue walking north-west before turning north-east to descend steeply through woods to Tsarein

*This pass has had different names over the years. In the early part of the last century it was known as Col de la Croix des Trente Pas but for decades it has been called Croix de la Cha until the most recent LK, which refers to it as La Croix de l'Achia. Presumably Cha was derived from the local dialect words Chat or Chaz meaning a saw or ragged crest. The strange corruption l'Achia would seem to be a result of the LK attempts to spell names as they sound; it is not used here.

The Tungelschuss

Langermatte

The Lake at Derborence

Les Diablerets

Lenk railway station and the Hotel Wilsdtrubel

Below the Simmenfälle

Vordere Wispile

The Geltenbach en route to the Gelten Hut

Lötschenpass Hut

Iffigsee and the descent to Iffigenalp

Cabane Rambert and the Petit Muveran

Glacier and Lac de la Forcla

The Arête de l'Arpille

View south from the Col des Audannes

Plan des Roses en route to the Rawilpass

Rawilpass looking back at the Col des Eaux Froides

Alpine Buttercup

Spring Gentian

Common Spotted Orchid

Alpine Lousewort

Round-leaved Pennycress

Bernese Alps Western Touring Route

Sunrise at the Cabane Rambert

Dent Blanche and Matterhorn behind the Pointe de Chemo

Grand Combin

Mont Blanc

The hamlet of Ferden in the Lötschental

Rezligletscherseeli and the Tierbergsattel

Descending to Stiereläger from the Wildstrubel Hut

Descending to Iffigenalp from the Rawilpass

Wildstrubel and the Glacier de la Plaine Morte

Rawilseelini from the Tierbergsattel

The Oeschinensee

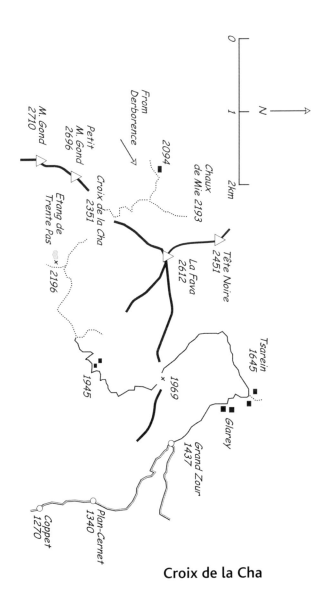

Croix de la Cha

(1,645m, 6¼ hours). There is no accommodation to be found here so descend to Grand Zour (1,437m, 6¾ hours); Plan-Cernet (1,340m, 7¼ hours) or Coppet (1,270m, 7½ hours) to find somewhere to stay. For public transport details, see Appendix C.

Col du Sanetsch to Wildstrubel Hut

This exciting and well-marked stretch takes two days and is conveniently split at the Cabane des Audannes.

Col du Sanetsch to the Cabane des Audannes via the Col des Audannes

From Cabane de Prarochet

Distance	14km
Ascent	779m
Descent	823m
Time	5¼ hours

From Auberge du Barrage

Distance	14km
Ascent	997m
Descent	553m
Time	5¼ hours

From the Cabane de Prarochet follow the description in Stage 3a to the Col du Sanetsch (2,252m, 1 hour). From the Auberge du Barrage walk up the road using paths to cut across some hairpins to reach the col in much the same time. Ascend the Arête de l'Arpille on moraine and grass to 400m beyond spot height 2,652m (2½ hours) – a little vertiginous in places. Descend slightly across a scree slope to arrive at the head of a narrow valley close to spot height 2,598m and go north-east, marker poles then cairns, to a little north of spot height 2,580m (2¾ hours). Here a path descends to the valley of the Grand' Gouilles and a lake at 2,471m (3¼ hours). Cross the outlet stream east of the lake, signpost, and ascend the slope that rises to the ridge between spot height 2,988m and spot height 2,886m. At one point the path makes a long leg to the north to turn a rock-band before continuing towards spot height 2,886m. The going becomes quite steep and a fixed rope aids the ascent to a subsidiary col at roughly 2,840m. Here there is a choice between a scramble protected by a fixed rope or a short descent to a ladder to reach the Col des Audannes (2,850m, 4½ hours).

Go down a few zig-zags to reach easy ground and continue south-east to La Selle (2,709m). Ahead lies a lunar landscape, the Cirque des Audannes, with immense fields of limestone and scattered rocks of various shapes and

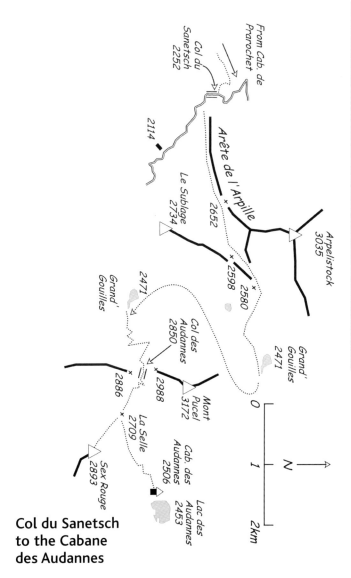

Col du Sanetsch to Wildstrubel Hut

From Cab de Prarochet

Col du Sanetsch 2252

2114

Arête de l'Arpille

Le Sublage 2734

2652

2598

2580

Arpelistock 3035

Grand' Gouilles

2471

Grand' Gouilles 2471

Col des Audannes 2850

2886

2988

Mont Pucel 3172

La Selle 2709

Sex Rouge 2893

Cab. des Audannes 2506

Lac des Audannes 2453

0   1   2Km

N

Col du Sanetsch to the Cabane des Audannes

> ## Sex* Rouge (2,893m)
> An easy ascent from La Selle goes via the north-west ridge, following traces of a path (30 minutes). A viewpoint beyond the summit (2,884m), cairn and cross, affords a stunning panorama. In the early season do not walk on the snow cornices along the crest. Up and down adds less than an hour to the trip.

colours. Descend east across occasional snowfields on a well-marked path. The cabin is hidden from view until the last moment when it appears on a little terrace above the Lac des Audannes (5¼ hours).

Cabane des Audannes to Wildstrubel Hut and Iffigenalp

Distance	10km
Ascent	744m
Descent	459m
Time	5½ hours

Although it is not far to the Plan des Roses, across the Col des Eaux Froides, and the height gain is modest, it takes longer than might be imagined because of the nature of the terrain. The area between the Col and the Plan des Roses consists of limestone lapiés, sheets of hard limestone with intricate channels formed by rainwater or melting snow dissolving the calcium carbonate in the rock when it is exposed on the surface. Walking on this terrain is great fun but demands constant

attention. Once across this interesting ground the way becomes very easy.

From the hut descend to the Lac des Audannes (2,453m) cross a marshy area using stepping stones and follow the path to the Col des Eaux Froides (2,648m, 45 minutes). Descend easily on a well-made path just above the bottom of a narrow valley. Soon cross to the left side of the valley, spot height 2,457m, and traverse an attractive grassy area to reach a small stone-field. Cross this and start to gain height across lapiés marked with poles and flashes; there's a fine view of the Lac de Tseuzier. Passing a signpost, where a difficult descent leads to Tseuzier, the path arrives at the Lac de Ténéhet (2,440m, 1¼ hours). Follow the marked path, still making height on lapiés, then start to lose some height, pass another junction to Tseuzier (signposted) and eventually escape from the beds of limestone to grass, flowers and cattle, 2¾ hours. It is easy going from here to a small lake (2,367m, 3¼ hours), where a well-beaten path leads to

---

This strange appellation for a mountain is ubiquitous in this part of Switzerland. It occurs in many variants such as Sasse, Sciex, and Six and is derived from the Latin saxum, *rock.*

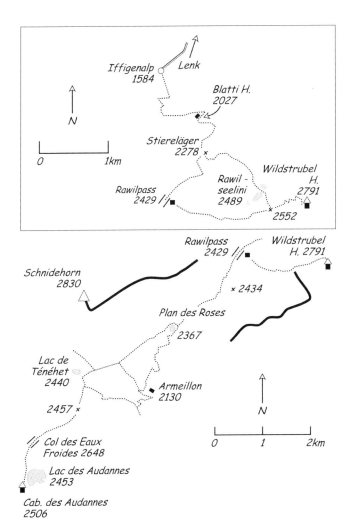

Cabane des Audannes to Wildstrubel Hut and Iffigenalp

the Rawilpass (2,429m, 4 hours). Turn right at the chalet and follow a marked path to the junction with the path from Iffigenalp just beyond

the Rawilseelini (2,552m, 4½ hours). Now zig-zag up the right side of a stony rib to reach the Wildstrubel Hut (2,791m, 5½ hours).

Descent to Iffigenalp

If you have passed several nights in huts it may be time to luxuriate in a hotel. The Gasthaus at Iffigenalp has a number of charming double rooms or there is a bus to Lenk. From the Rawilpass descend easily north-east for about 750m on stable scree, where pleasant zig-zags lead to a junction at Stiereläger (2,278m, 4¼ hours). A good path continues under a military cableway past the Blatti Hut (2,027m, 4¾ hours) – a shepherds' stone-built byre, no accommodation – before turning west, under the cableway again and down a short rock-band. A rather exposed but protected section passes by a waterfall until easy ground is reached and the path cuts through an area of scrubby bushes and trees before crossing a river to arrive at Iffigenalp (1,584m, 5½ hours).

Wildhorn Hut to the Wildstrubel Hut via the Schnidejoch

Distance	10km
Ascent	877m
Descent	389m
Time	5¾ hours

This is a useful route for walkers who have taken the easier way from the Auberge du Barrage or Cabane de Prarochet towards Iffigenalp but wish to get back into higher, more rugged terrain. Thirty years ago, the Schnidejoch had to be approached across the Chilchli Glacier but the glacier has retreated sufficiently to allow a passage to be made beneath its shrunken snout.

From the back of the hut follow a small path, cairned, across a stream (may be dry) and work up easily to a moraine crest. Follow the ridge, steep in parts, towards a small peak, Chilchli, ignoring cairns to the right at about 2,475m until you reach the edge of the Chilchli Glacier, around 2,600m, (45 minutes). Ignore any tracks that might be seen leading on to the glacier and turn east to follow a cairned path beneath its snout. The ground here is not particularly good but in 15 minutes the way turns south-east and the going becomes much better. In the early part of the season there may be several large

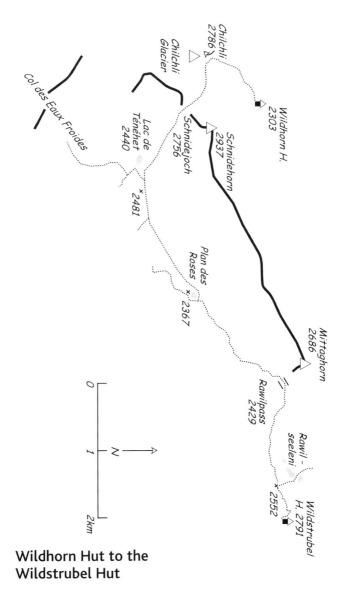

**Wildhorn Hut to the
Wildstrubel Hut**

snow plaques to cross to reach the col but these are not part of the glacier and are usually safe to walk on unroped; no real need for an ice-axe. Aim for the obvious opening of the Schnidejoch (2,756m, 1½ hours).

The descent is straightforward and marked by small cairns and red flashes although these may be obscured by snow just below the col. The path does not follow the bottom of the valley but stays up on the north, left, side. After a short steep section it soon becomes very easy going and fine views of the Lac de Ténéhet and, further away, the Lac de Tseuzier open out. Continue down following the marks until the way joins the path from the Col des Eaux Froides, east of Lac de Ténéhet (2 hours). Now follow the route described on page 68 across rough limestone lapiés marked with red and white flashes and poles, to easier ground, which leads to a small lake (2,367m, 3½ hours) where a well-beaten path crosses Plan des Roses to the Rawilpass (2,429m, 4¼ hours). Turn right at the chalet and follow a marked path to the junction with the path from Iffigenalp, just beyond the Rawilseelini, 2,552m, 4¾ hours. Now zig-zag up the right side of a stony rib to the Wildstrubel Hut, 2,791m, 5¾ hours.

Wildstrubel Hut to Engstligenalp

Two variants of the magnificent passage between the Wildstrubel Hut and Engstligenalp are described here. The first can be done in one day across the Tierbergsattel and Ammertenpass. The second takes two days starting with an ascent of the Wildstrubel, descending to the Flueseeli Hut or the Gasthaus Rezliberg followed by the Ammertenpass.

Via Tierbergsattel and Ammertenpass

Distance	18km
Ascent	1,229m
Descent	2,068m
Time	8¼ hours

This is an excellent outing for a strong party. There is no technical difficulty but it is a long day, about 9 hours with stops, and after a spell of bad weather the south side of the Ammertenpass can be very difficult.

From the hut descend a stony rib on its south flank to a junction at spot height 2,552m where the right fork is taken to the Rawilseelini (2,489m). Pass between the north-ernmost pair of lakes and follow the signed path to the Tierbergsattel (2,654m, 1 hour). The first few metres of descent are on rather

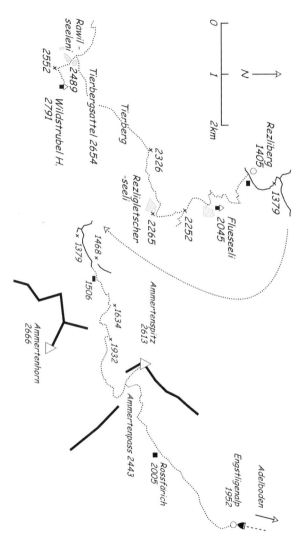

Wildstrubel Hut to Engstligenalp

poor, loose moraine, and a little care is needed, but after a very short distance the problems disappear. Descend easily towards a flat, slightly boggy area close to spot height 2,326m (1½ hours). The way now turns east and makes a little height between limestone outcrops before traversing across a grassy hillside and descending towards the Rezligletscherseeli. After crossing two plank bridges the path ascends rough ground somewhat west of north. There is no path shown on LK but it is well marked on the ground with paint flashes and large poles.

Once over a minor col descend on roughish terrain past spot height 2,252m where a path leads to the Wildstrubel. A steep move down a small nose on the ridge leads to a grassy slope where a path passes a very small lake to reach Flueseeli (2,045m, 2½ hours). The descent to Rezliberg works its way down a steep cliff in a series of zig-zags, several of which are protected by a fixed chain, until the path reaches a meadow which is only a short stroll from the Gasthaus Rezliberg (1,405m, 3¼ hours). This inn is also known as the Restaurant Siebenbrunnen, a name

deriving from springs close by – of which there used to be seven – that form the source of the river Simme. Continue eastwards past the inn to a bridge (1,379m, 3½ hours). Cross the river and, after 150m, take a right fork on a farm track to a further junction at spot height 1,468m (3¾ hours) – the signpost suggests a rather fast time to the pass. Go right, cross the Ammerten stream and enter a wood by a building at 1,506m. Gain height easily, recross the stream at spot height 1,634m (4½ hours), and follow it for about 400m before working round a rock bluff past the Ammerten Hut (private) to a fine viewpoint. Gain more height to spot height 1,932m (5½ hours), where the path continues by the stream for a while before turning north-east and working its way up increasingly steep ground. Some care is needed in places until, at around 2,200m, the gradient eases and a final set of zig-zags is followed by an amusing traverse to the Ammertenpass (2,443m, 7½ hours).

The descent is easy and well-marked with red and white flashes. There are some clear short cuts and variations but all ways lead to a large, flat plain where paths cross a number of streams and marshy patches to Engstligenalp (1,952m, 8¼ hours). Choice of accommodation here or take the cable-car down to Unter dem Birg and bus to Adelboden.

Ammertenspitz (2,613m)

It takes only 30–40 minutes to climb this small peak on the Ammertengrat and it is well worth the effort for the views.

The Wildstrubel and descent to Flueseeli and Rezliberg

Distance	13km
Ascent	596m
Descent	1,982m
Time	5¾ hours

The south-west flank of the Wildstrubel forms the highest part of the rim enclosing the north side of the Glacier de la Plaine Morte. In summer conditions the ascent from the Wildstrubel Hut is little more than a walk in about 3 hours. The scenery is exceptionally fine with magnificent views from the summit.

From the hut go south-east on rocks and scree – often snow-covered – to a small col, Weisshornlücke (2,852m, 15 minutes). Descend across occasional snow patches passing west of the Pointe de Vatseret to spot height 2,741m (30 minutes) and descending a little to the Glacier de la Plaine Morte. Once on the glacier it is normally best to go east for 2km before trending slightly left to reach the shaly toe of the flank below and somewhat right of the summit line (about 2,800m, 1½ hours). A small path leads up to a knoll (2,910m); continue in many short zig-zags somewhat left of the shoulder formed on this flank. A broad crest is joined in the upper part (often snowy) and is followed all the way

to the summit (3,243m, 3 hours).

To descend to the Flueseeli Hut and the Gasthaus Rezliberg reverse the ascent route, passing a faint path on the right at about 3,000m to a better path on the right just above spot height 2,910m. Take this and descend north-west, initially on rather poor scree but the going soon improves. Pass below a small rise, 2,505m, to spot height 2,415m (4¼ hours), before descending steeply through a weakness in a rock-band to a junction at 2,252m and so to Flueseeli (2,045m, 4¾ hours). The descent to Rezliberg works its way down a steep cliff in a series of zig-zags several of which are protected by a fixed chain until the path reaches a meadow which is only a short stroll from the Gasthaus Rezliberg (1,405m, 5¾ hours).

If no accommodation is available there is a bus to Lenk from the road-head below the Simmenfälle, which is easily reached in 45 minutes along a well-marked track. The next day continue to Engstligenalp following the description in the previous route.

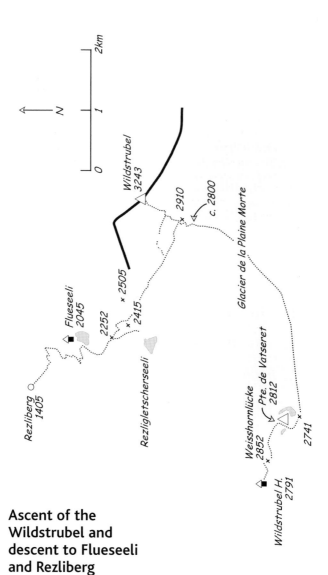

Ascent of the Wildstrubel and descent to Flueseeli and Rezliberg

Part Three
Day Walks

It is all too easy when doing a tour like this to keep pushing on and to miss out on the pleasure of just being in the Alps and idling away a day taking in the atmosphere and recharging oneself. To many people, there is a particular pleasure in spending a couple of nights in the same place – getting some washing done, pottering around the bakery or the delicatessen, enjoying a cold beer or a glass of wine on a hotel terrace. One does not need advice on the best way to do this. However, some people (and I must confess to being in their company) like a day off but are not practised at doing nothing. For those who enjoy walking with a virtually empty rucksack I have included some suggestions for day walks.

Walks at Villars

From Villars a rack railway winds up from the central bus and tram station as far as the Col de Bretaye saddle (1,806m) and a cableway rises to the Roc d'Orsay (1,950m). Both sites offer refreshments and numerous pleasant walks, two of which are described here.

Le Chamossaire and four lakes

Distance	9km
Ascent	447m
Descent	447m
Time	3½ hours

This walk is not in the tourist office brochure, presumably because the descent from Le Chamossaire is narrow, steep and exposed in its initial stages. It's an excellent outing but not recommended in damp conditions.

Starting from Bretaye take the obvious track to the Roc d'Orsay terminus (1,950m, 30 minutes). Follow a piste through a cutting and go up a grassy slope past a large pylon to a terrace at the top. Step up right through a small gate to the highest point (2,112m, 1 hour). There is a magnificent panorama across the Rhône Valley from the Mont Blanc range to the western part of the Pennine Alps. Return to the terrace and traverse north along a small but clear path, narrow in places, descending and crossing steep ground only a few metres below the ridge crest. Cross over a little saddle and up to spot height 2,085m for sensational views. Continue with interest just below the crest to where the path plunges down 60m at 35 degrees with several rocky bits (very slippery in damp conditions) until easier ground is reached by spot height 2,010m (1½ hours).

A good path descends east towards spot height 1,712m but a small detour affords a better view of the Lac de Bretaye and Lac Noir. So, after about 300m take a vague branch right, descending towards a line of trees, through which the faint path goes in a cutting, then cross a small open stretch into a few trees again, soon reaching a sharp turn right (south-west). Now much improved the path goes down more steeply and in a curve south-east to pass above the Lac de Bretaye to the Crêta cowsheds (2 hours). Here a track leads north-east to spot height 1,712m, but a nice path branches off right past the Lac Noir then the marshy Entonnoir, and round Lac des Chavonnes, to join a rough road which leads to spot height 1,795m (2¾ hours). A good path leads back through woods and rough open

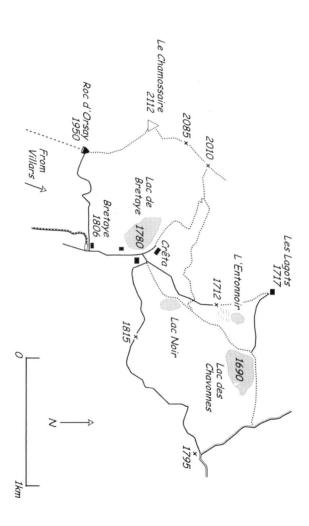

Le Chamossaire and four lakes

ground to near the Crêta buildings and so to Bretaye (1,806m, 3½ hours). You'll need transport back to Villars or you can descend on foot from Bretaye in 1½ hours, as described in the next route.

Tour de Chaux Ronde

Distance	15km
Ascent	229m
Descent	782m
Time	4 hours

Apart from the pull up to L'Encrène this is as near as one can get to a walk on the flat in the Alps.

From the terminus at Bretaye go south for about 200m where a broad track forks off left. Take this and contour round the hillside, past spot height 1,776m, until the track divides (1,780m, 30 minutes). Follow a path left and pass just above the main group of buildings at Ensex (1,787m, 45 minutes). Grazing cattle can sometimes obscure the paths hereabouts but it is not difficult to find the way to the small col, L'Encrène (1,936m, 1¼ hours) which lies east of spot height 1,993m. A nice path descends on grass through scrubby bushes to join a stony track. Turn left at the track and make your way to the busy farm at Perche (1,790m, 1½ hours). Pass between the farm buildings and pick up a faint path (sometimes a little muddy) that runs beneath a

cableway and eventually joins a track north of Conche (2 hours). A good track leads to Bretaye lake, a café and a pleasant restaurant and, further along, the Bretaye railway station and hotel (1,806m, 2½ hours).

To descend on foot to Villars follow the track south from Bretaye once more – but this time ignore the left turning – keeping the railway track on your right until, 450m beyond the halt at 1,759m, the way passes beneath it. The path across the wooded hillside has some seats which make a nice place to stop for lunch and, somewhat incongruously, watch golfers driving-off on the course below. Soon the track crosses the railway again and arrives at Col de Soud (1,524m, 3¼ hours) where refreshments are usually available. Turn left (south) and continue on a track through woods. After about 12 minutes reach a metalled road where, just beyond Le Sex (1,433m, 3½ hours), a path breaks off right and zig-zags down through trees to a main road. Turn right and, crossing a railway bridge, come into Villars (1,253m, 4 hours).

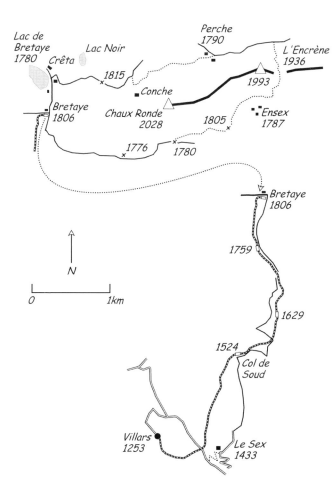

Tour de Chaux Ronde
and descent to Villars

Walks from Iffigenalp and Lenk

Three outings are suggested here. The first is an ascent of the Pointe de la Plaine Morte; the second a tour of high lakes; the third visits the Wildhorn Hut and crosses two passes before returning to to Iffigenalp.

Pointe de la Plaine Morte

Distance	15km
Ascent	1,565m
Descent	1,565m
Time	7³/₄ hours

Take the path opposite the inn at Iffigenalp, cross the river and turn right (signposted). The path goes up in forest and gradually steepens into zig-zags which climb through rock barriers. A long traverse east in impressive rock surroundings leads past a waterfall before reaching the Blatti Hut (2,027m, 1¹/₄ hours). Continue steeply over the Blattihubel shoulder to a fork on a small plateau called Stiereläger (2,278m, 2 hours). Take the left branch over less steep ground and ascend on scree with small snow fields to another fork just before the three Rawilseeleni lakes (2,489m, 2¹/₂ hours). Continue ahead and pass through a neck between the two largest of the three lakes to reach, in 250m, a junction with the path from the Rawilpass. Turn sharp left and start zig-zagging up the right side of a stony rib – large snow patches in early season – to reach the

Wildstrubel Hut (2,791m, 3¹/₂ hours). If you have to return to Lenk, now is the moment to decide if there is time to continue to the Plaine Morte and get back to Iffigenalp in time for the last bus. If in doubt, cross the Tierbergsattel instead and descend to Simmenfälle; see the next route.

For the Plaine Morte go south-east from the hut on rocks and scree – often snow-covered – to a small col, Weisshornlücke (2,852m, 3³/₄ hours). Descend across occasional snow patches passing west of the Pointe de Vatseret to spot height 2,741m (4 hours). An easy moraine and frozen snow slope leads directly to the Pointe de la Plaine Morte (2,927m, 4³/₄ hours), where there are excellent views of the Wildstrubel and, to the south, the Pennine Alps.

The glacier itself is one of the remarkable sights of the Wildstrubel massif and reasonably safe to walk on, provided there is no snow to hide what crevasses there are. However, be careful of the steep ice slope above the moraine lake to the east of the Pointe de Vatseret. The return to Iffigenalp reverses the above and takes about 3 hours.

Walks from Iffigenalp and Lenk

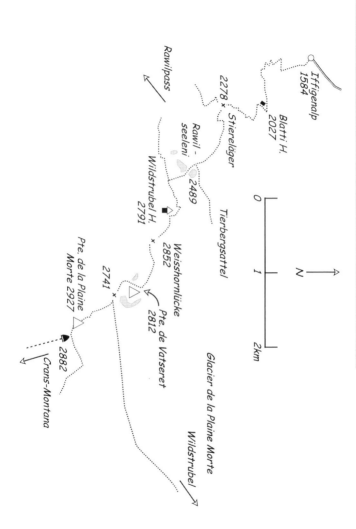

Pointe de la Plaine Morte

A tour of high lakes from Iffigenalp

Returning to Iffigenalp

Distance	17km
Ascent	1,561m
Descent	1,561m
Time	7¾ hours

Returning to Simmenfälle

Distance	14km
Ascent	1,070m
Descent	1,549m
Time	5¾ hours

This walk is best suited to those staying in Lenk since they can return to their accommodation without having to complete a full circuit. From Iffigenalp (reached by bus from Lenk) follow the previous route as far as the three Rawilseelini lakes (2,489m, 2½ hours). At the signpost fork left and follow the obvious path to the Tierbergsattel (2,654m, 3 hours). The way ahead is quite clear and in the far distance one can see the Flueseeli.

For just the first few metres of descent the ground is rather poor, loose moraine, and a little care is needed, but after a very short distance the problems disappear. The way is well marked and there are no route finding problems as you descend easily towards a flat, slightly boggy area close to spot height 2,326m (3½ hours). The way now turns east and makes a little height

between limestone outcrops before traversing across a grassy hillside and descending towards the Rezligletscherseeli. After crossing two plank bridges the path ascends rough ground somewhat to the west of north. There is no path shown on LK map but it is well marked on the ground with paint flashes and large poles.

Once over a minor col descend on roughish terrain past spot height 2,252m where a path leads to the Wildstrubel. A steep move down a small nose on the ridge leads to a grassy slope where a path passes a very small lake to reach Flueseeli (2,045m, 4¼ hours). The descent to Rezliberg works its way down a steep cliff in a series of zig-zags, several of which are protected by a fixed chain, until the path reaches a meadow, which is only a short stroll from the Gasthaus Rezliberg (1,405m, 5 hours).

To return to Lenk follow the sign-posted track to the Simmenfälle and take the path alongside the torrent to the roadhead (1,105m, 5¾ hours). There is a bus service from here to Lenk; last bus 17:25.

To return to Iffigenalp, take the track then paths to Langer (1,705m, 6¼ hours) and Langermatte (1,857m, 6¾ hours) before descending through Ritz (1,739m) to Iffigenalp (1,584m, 7¾ hours).

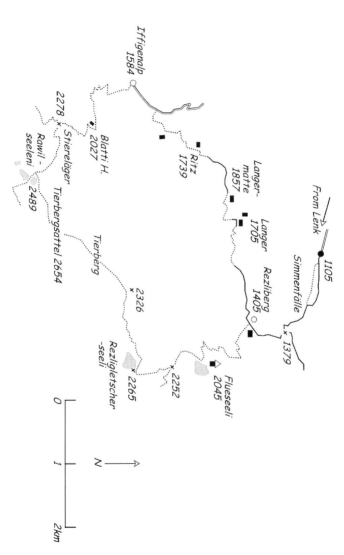

Iffigenalp
1584

2278

Rawil -
seeleni
2489

Stiereläger

Blatti H.
2027

Tierbergsattel 2654

Ritz
1739

Tierberg

Langer-
matte
1857

2326
×

Langer
1705

Rezliberg
1405

From Lenk

Simmenfälle

1105

× 1379

Rezligletscher
-seeli

× 2265

× 2252

Flueseeli
2045

0   1   2km

N →

A tour of high lakes

Schnidejoch and Rawilpass

Distance	17km
Ascent	1,234m
Descent	1,234m
Time	7 hours

The passage between the Wildhorn Hut and the Wildstrubel Hut across the Schnidejoch has already been described on page 70. From Iffigenalp one can make a delightful circular tour past Iffigsee to the Wildhorn Hut and across the Schnidejoch to the Lac de Ténéhet where the route from the Cabane des Audannes, see page 68, is followed to the Rawilpass and Iffigenalp. This gives a good feeling of the terrain south of the Wildhorn without the need to experience it with a full rucksack. The lighter rucksack is reflected in the times given here which are a little faster than the previous routes would suggest.

From Iffigenalp reverse Stage 4 to the col just above Iffigsee (2,086m, 1¼ hours). Traverse above the lake turning gently to the south until the Wildhorn Hut comes into sight on a small rise at the end of a barren cwm. Cross easy ground and ascend a few zig-zags to the hut (2,303m, 2 hours). Now take a path from the back of the hut to a moraine crest which is followed to the edge of the Chilchli Glacier (2,600m, 2¾ hours). Traverse east beneath the snout of the glacier for 15 minutes until better ground leads south-east to the Schnidejoch (2,756m, 3½ hours).

The descent route is marked by small cairns and red flashes, and soon joins the path from the Col des Eaux Froides (4 hours). Somewhat hard going across rough limestone lapiés leads to an area of grass and flowers where a slight ascent brings one to a small lake (2,367m, 5 hours) from where a well-beaten path crosses Plan des Roses to the Rawilpass (2,429m, 5½ hours).

Descend easily to a junction at Stiereläger (2,278m, 5¾ hours). Continue past the Blatti Hut (2,027m, 6¼ hours), before turning west down a short rock-band and crossing a rather exposed but protected section by a waterfall until easy ground is reached and the path cuts through an area of scrubby bushes and trees before crossing a river to arrive at Iffigenalp (1,584m, 7 hours). To do this you need the first bus from Lenk at 09:13 to Iffigenalp which reaches Iffigenalp at 09:40. The last bus back to Lenk leaves Iffigenalp at 17:45 in the high season.

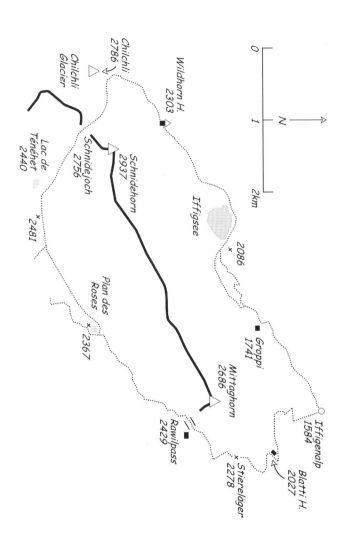

Schnidejoch and
Rawilpass

Walks at Leukerbad

Leukerbad is a relaxing place to idle away a pleasant rest-day or enjoy a less challenging day walk. There are many excursions from the resort and two possibilities are described here. The first, an easy circular walk as far as the chapel at Flüekapelle, passes through some delightful Alpine scenery and towards the end there is a fine view of the Ferdenpass, a good ski-touring route in winter, between Leukerbad and the Lötschental but rarely used by walkers. The second walk ascends the Torrenthorn with the possibility of an airy traverse to return to Leukerbad.

Flüekapelle

Distance	13km
Ascent	668m
Descent	668m
Time	4¼ hours

From the centre of Leukerbad follow signs to the Gemmi cable-car station. At a water trough with a rather fine bronze statue turn right, signed to Clabinualp. Follow a narrow lane between houses and work uphill north-east to reach a track just beyond spot height 1,474m (15 minutes). Take this and, ignoring forks left and right, gain height over several streams across the broad hillside of Clabinualp (1,861m, 1½ hours). The path continues to rise as it passes a small tarn and arrives at another series of stream crossings beyond spot height 1,942m. At this point there are fine views of the Torrenthorn and Majinghorn and the sensational path that descends beneath them (see the following route). The path gradu-

ally gets closer to the river Dala until it reaches a crossing at Flüekapelle (2,070m, 2½ hours).

To return to Leukerbad, cross the river and traverse, crossing yet more streams, to Flüealp (2,040m) where the track continues past a junction with the steep descent path from the Torrenthorn at spot height 2,052m. Cross the Flüebach at spot height 2,029m to reach a small cluster of buildings (not shown on LK25) at 1,975m (3 hours). Here, a footpath descends steeply through some woods and across Majingalp past spot height 1,769m to reach a track by the Flüebach. Turn right (north-east), cross the river at spot height 1,653m and follow a track south-west over two more bridges until a path leads back across the river (1,543m, 3¾ hours). Alternatively take a right fork, instead of crossing the river, to rejoin the ascent path. In either case, continue walking without difficulty to Leukerbad (1,402m, 4¼ hours).

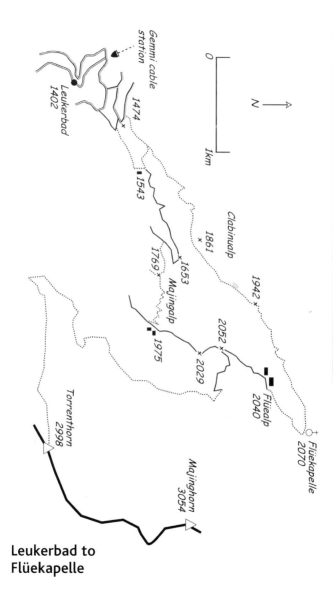

Leukerbad to
Flüekapelle

The Torrenthorn

Descending to Rinder Hut

Distance	9km
Ascent	688m
Descent	688m
Time	3¼ hours

Descending to Leukerbad

Distance	15km
Ascent	748m
Descent	1,656m
Time	6 hours

This is an easy ascent – in the 1880s tourists often went nearly all the way on horseback – with excellent views. Eastwards one can see the Jungfrau, Blümlisalp and the Lötschentaler Breithorn, and to the south the Matterhorn, Weisshorn and Dom. Although LK shows a path from the cable-car terminus at the Rinder Hut (2,310m) to the Hotel Torrenthorn ✳, continuing towards the Torrenthorn, it is in poor condition especially above the hotel. The best approach is to follow the service track to the hotel from the cable-car terminus as far as spot height 2,449m, go sharp left, under a cableway and take a right fork, signposted to the Torrenthorn. A grass slope, then a rough path lead to spot height 2,562m (45 minutes). There is a signpost and a faint path to the left here. Fork right and zig-zag up a nose before less steep ground leads

under a cableway to spot height 2,748m (1¼ hours). A stiff pull up to the forepeak, 2,889m (1¾ hours) is followed by an easy gradient on a cairned path to the summit (2,998m, 2 hours). The last section can have large snow plaques.

Difficult descent to Leukerbad

The easiest way down is to reverse the ascent and take the cable-car, but it is more exciting to take the airy trail to Flüealp – a very exposed path, vertiginous and not for the faint-hearted. From the summit reverse the ascent described above to the junction close to the top of a cableway, about 160m beyond spot height 2,449m (2¾ hours). Turn right (north). Initially, the path is firm on the grassy hillside but soon, after a zig-zag downward, it breaches the face of a shaly cliff and becomes narrow in places. After about 600m, near spot height 2,385m, the footing improves although the narrowness remains as the path crosses a gully and ascends for some distance working in and out of re-entrants with more or less exposure until good ground is reached at spot height 2,176m (4½ hours). Descend easily to spot height 2,052m and follow the previous route through Majingalp to Leukerbad (1,402m, 6 hours).

✳ *This large, barracks-like hotel is usually closed in summer and serves only winter skiing.*

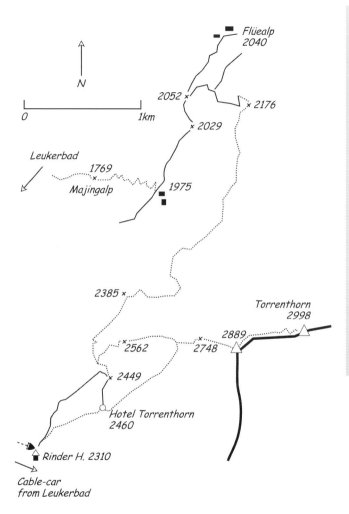

N

Leukerbad

Flüealp
2040

2052 ×

× 2176

× 2029

1769
×
Majingalp

1975

2385 ×

Torrenthorn
2998

× 2562

× 2748

2889

× 2449

Hotel Torrenthorn
2460

Rinder H. 2310

Cable-car
from Leukerbad

0   1km

Torrenthorn and
descent to Leukerbad

Walks at Kandersteg

Kandersteg merits a day or two for exploration. The tourist office has several leaflets outlining a variety of walks from the village, three of which are described in detail here. LK1248 or a Kandersteg walking map is needed for the walk to the Blümlisalp Hut.

Oeschinensee and Blümlisalp Hut

Going to Oeschinensee

Distance	6km
Ascent	0m
Descent	506m
Time	1½ hours

Going to Blümlisalp Hut

Distance	15km
Ascent	1,200m
Descent	1,200m
Time	6 hours

Judging by the number of posters depicting the Oeschinensee it would seem to be to Kandersteg what the Matterhorn is to Zermatt but it has the advantage that it can be reached by a chair-lift and a downhill walk. Those wishing for a more energetic day can continue to the Blümlisalp Hut and enjoy remarkable views of hanging glaciers on the Blümlisalp massif.

From the top of the chair-lift follow a signposted track east to Läger (1,659m, 15 minutes). It is only a short distance through trees to the edge of the lake. Although it is not possible to make a circumnavigation, paths go both ways here. Clockwise, a rising path leads eventually to the Blümlisalp Hut; anticlockwise the way leads to the restaurants at the western end of the lake (30 minutes). To return to Kandersteg either take the path that descends by the service road or return to spot height 1,671m where a steep path follows the line of the cableway.

For the Blümlisalp Hut continue on the well-marked path north of the lake to Unterbergli (1,767m, 1 hour). The path zig-zags up to a rock step with fixed rails to arrive at the Oberbergli chalets (1,978m, 1½ hours), where you'll find refreshments. Cross a stream and follow a path that zig-zags up to a lateral moraine, spot height 2,324m. Walk along the top of the moraine, with good views of the Blümlisalp Glacier to the right, making height easily between fine cliffs to a shaly slope below the Hohtürli saddle (2,549m, 3 hours). Shortly beyond this point the path divides. Although there is a cairn about 100m along the lower (right) branch this is not the way; fork left and work up to a rockface, pass beneath this and gain a little more height to the Hohtürli, then

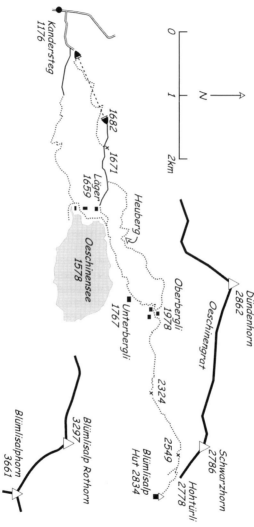

The map shows walking routes with the following labelled features:

- Kandersteg 1176
- 1682
- 1671
- Läger 1659
- Oeschinensee 1578
- Heuberg
- Unterbergli 1767
- Oberbergli 1978
- Dündenhorn 2862
- Oeschinengrat
- Schwarzhorn 2786
- 2324
- 2549
- Blümlisalp Hut 2834
- Hohtürli 2778
- Blümlisalp Rothorn 3297
- Blümlisalphorn 3661
- Scale: 0 — 1 — 2km, N

Oeschinensee and Blümlisalp
Hut from Kandersteg

turn right to the Blümlisalp Hut
(2,834m, 4 hours).

In descent reverse the above as far
as Oberbergli (1 hour) then take the
upper path through Heuberg
(1½ hours) for excellent views of the
lake. It is 30 minutes from here to
the top of the chair-lift (1,682m,
2 hours).

Allmenalp, First and the Golitschenpass to Kandersteg

Distance	11km
Ascent	866m
Descent	1,413m
Time	5¼ hours

The cable-car from outside
Kandersteg to Allmenalp, at the edge
of a huge, grassy cwm above the
village opens up a number of high-
level walks. The route described here
demands a little effort to reach the
summit of First but this unpreten-
tious peak provides an extensive
panorama including Mont Blanc, the
Matterhorn and the northern
Bernese peaks.

The cable-car station is south of the
village, close by spot height 1,181m
(see page 50 for details). The rather
old, eight-man car rises steeply, close
to a sheer rock face with amazing
views of a waterfall. Having regained
one's breath at the top station
follow the main trail west, ignore a

path that cuts off left and cross a
fence where a second path goes off
to the left. Continue for 200m to a
junction with a path to Obere
Allmen (30 minutes). Keep right
(signposted) but soon turn north-
east on a small path that ascends a
boggy area on nicely positioned
stepping stones. Cross a stile and
make height more easily to Steintal
(2,027m, 45 minutes). Move up right
behind the chalet then immediately
sharp left; gradually turn northwards
and work up steepening ground in
zig-zags to First (2,549m, 2¾ hours)
where there are magnificent views in
all directions.

The narrow ridge between First and
Stand is avoided by descending
across the west face of Howang. The
first 30m of descent are protected
by a wire as is a second exposed
section, then easy ground leads to a
junction at spot height 2,280m
before a short ascent to Stand
(2,320m, 3¼ hours). This is a good
place to stop for lunch.

To reach the Golitschenpass,
descend the north-west ridge for
about 120m (vertical) then contour
east in an arc beside a limestone
rock face to the col (2,180m,
3½ hours). On the eastern side
descend in a series of large zig-zags
to a chalet at 1,833m (4 hours,
simple refreshments). From the
chalet the path turns right (south-
west) then south-east (take care

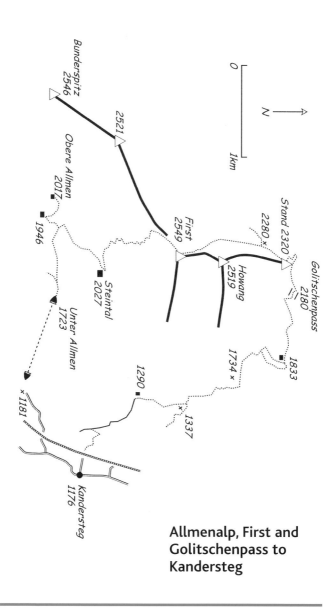

Bunderspitz
2546

2521

Obere Allmen
2017

1946

First
2549

Stand 2320

2280 x

Howang
2519

Golitschenpass
2180

Steintal
2027

Unter Allmen
1723

1734 x

1833

x 1181

1290

x 1337

Kandersteg
1176

**Allmenalp, First and
Golitschenpass to
Kandersteg**

Bernese Alps Western Touring Route

with route finding) and descends through trees, crosses a stream and turns a spur beneath spot height 1,734m on the right. Continue steeply to the valley to reach a junction by a gate and signpost (1,337m, 4½ hours). Here there is a choice of paths to Kandersteg; the easiest way is to follow signs to the station, initially on a path with yellow flashes then a track by a building at 1,290m (4¾ hours). Continue through woodland to Kandersteg which is reached in 5¼ hours.

Allmenalp, Usser Üschene, Kandersteg

Distance	10km
Ascent	72m
Descent	619m
Time	2¼ hours

This is an ideal walk to fill in a half day. It is nearly all downhill, offers several opportunities for refreshments, and has beautiful views of the Balmhorn, the Oeschinensee and the Blümlisalp range.

Start, as in the previous route, by taking the cable-car to Unter Allmen where the route via Ryharts and Usser Üschene is signposted.

Follow the main trail to the west but after about 800m fork left and descend slightly to a metal footbridge, cross the stream then climb slightly to arrive at the chalet-farm

of Allmenalp (15 minutes, refreshments available).

Continue south-east still slightly uphill to reach spot height. 1,795m. Now it is downhill all the way. A wide track leads in a southerly direction to chalets at Rhyarts (1,760m, 45 minutes). Here the track turns into a farm road and one can relax, striding gently downhill with superb views ahead and to the left. Eventually the road reaches a junction at Usser Üschene (1,595m, 1 hour, more refreshments).

Although it is possible to take the road all the way back to Eggeschwand and Kandersteg, a more attractive descent can be made by following the road past spot height 1,538m where, just after crossing a stream, a path leads off to the right. Take this and descend through trees by a fine torrent to a road junction where the way to Selden turns right. Continue ahead to the cable-car station at Eggeschwand. Refreshments and a bus service to Kandersteg can be found here. To walk to the village, follow the description on page 56.

96

Walks at Kandersteg

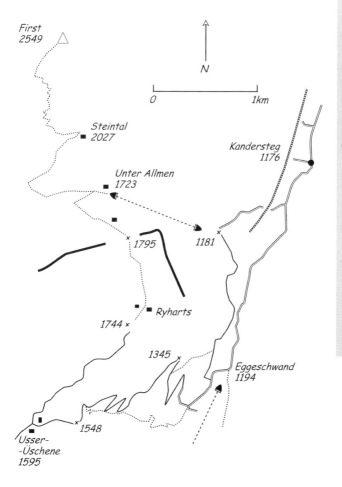

First
2549

Steintal
2027

Kandersteg
1176

Unter Allmen
1723

1181

1795

Ryharts

1744

1345

Eggeschwand
1194

1548

Usser-
-Üschene
1595

0   1km
N

Allmenalp, Usser
Üschene, Kandersteg

Appendix A
Hotels, Inns and Mountain Huts

All the valley bases are ski resorts with ample accommodation for summer visitors and it is not usually necessary to reserve rooms. However, in some parts of the walk there is only limited accommodation and it would be wise to book in advance.

Where comments are made regarding accommodation, food and the general level of helpfulness they are from first-hand experience or reports from good sources. But things can change from one year to another.

From the UK the dialling code is 00 41 and the leading zero is omitted.

Villars

Plenty of accommodation available in the summer as well as banks, shops and restaurants. Can be rather expensive so it pays to shop around. Les Papillons (1.5km from station) offers good value as does the Ecureuil (500m from station); Alpe Fleurie is more expensive but is opposite the station. The Rôtisserie des Alpes (opposite the Alpe Fleurie) is a good place to eat.

Du Golfe & Marie Loise ★★★★	024 495 24 77
Alpe Fleurie ★★★	024 495 34 64
Ecureuil ★★★	024 495 27 95
Sunstar Elite ★★★	024 496 39 00
Les Papillons ★	024 495 42 31

Bex

A substantial village with shops, banks and several hotels, two of which are members of the Swiss Tourist Association, Le Cèdre and Le St-Christophe, and three others that are recommended by the Swiss Tourist Office. Le Cèdre is very comfortable and has good food.

Le Cèdre ★★★★	024 463 01 11
Le St-Christophe ★★	024 485 29 77
La Fontaine	024 463 33 85
La Grappe d'Or	024 463 21 38
Hotel de Ville	024 463 20 82

La Barboleusaz

Not a lot here but a good hotel with lots of parking space. There's also an excellent mini-market, tea shop, bakers and a helpful tourist office.

La Crémaillère ★★   024 498 21 55

Les Plans sur Bex

Café-restaurant de l'Argentine   024 498 13 70
30 beds in rooms
Ancienne Poste   024 498 12 59
49 places in dormitories
Les Martinets   024 498 40 40
47 beds in rooms; 80 places in dormitories

Pont de Nant

Auberge Communale de Pont de Nant 024 498 14 95
10 beds in rooms; 45 places in dormitories
Arbalasse   024 463 02 66
32 places in one room and four dormitories

Solalex

Refuge de Solalex   024 498 15 95
11 places in dormitories

Anzeindaz

This is a delightful spot and both inns offer good value for money as well as a jeep service from Solalex. The food at the Refuge de la Tour is excellent.

Refuge de la Tour d'Anzeindaz   024 498 11 47
10 beds in four rooms and 70 places in dormitories
Refuge Giacomini   024 498 22 95
10 beds in rooms and 60 places in dormitories

Cabane Rambert

In a superb position below the Grand Muveran. Can get very busy.

Cabane Rambert SAC   027 207 11 22
50 places in dormitories

Derborence

The Refuge du Lac is beautifully positioned by the lake with a terrace for dining or an evening drink. The Auberge du Godet – at Godey – has been run by the same family for three generations and has a warm and friendly atmosphere with good mountain food.

Refuge du Lac   027 346 14 28
Dormitory accommodation only
Auberge du Godet   027 346 15 97
2.5km to east of Derborence. 30 places in rooms and a dormitory

Le Gîte de la Chaux de Derbon   027 207 17 33
3.5 km from Derborence on route from Cabane Rambert to Derborence. 10 places in a dormitory

Col du Sanetsch

There are several inns on the road between Sion and the Barrage du Sanetsch; unfortunately the Hotel du Sanetsch is no longer open. The Cabane de Prarochet is in a fascinating situation and the gardienne is proud of the evening menu with local wines and dishes. From south to north:

Auberge Beau Site at Coppet   027 346 19 03
Auberge du Plan Cernet   027 346 11 99
Around 29 places in dormitories
Auberge de Tsanfleuron at Grand Zour   027 346 30 96
A room for two and two dormitories for 12
Auberge du Barrage   033 755 12 32 or 027 395 24 10
Cabane de Prarochet   027 395 27 27
50 places in dormitories

Gsteig

There are two hotels in this attractive village. The Bären is the best value, although a little more expensive than the old fashioned Viktoria.
Hotel Bären   033 755 19 37
Hotel Viktoria   033 755 10 34

Gstaad

Hotels to suit most tastes, although it is difficult to find anything really inexpensive. The three suggested here are in, or close to, the traffic-free centre of the resort.

Gstaaderhof ★★★	033 748 63 63
Posthotel Rössli ★★★	033 748 42 42
Sporthotel Victoria ★★★	033 748 44 22

Lauenen

This is an extremely pretty village with many old wooden buildings and good views of the Wildhorn.

Wildhorn	033 765 30 12
In the village centre	
Alpenland ★★★	033 765 34 34

Adjacent to Rohr-Lauenensee nature reserve, close to gondola station at Rohr-Brügge

Gsteig to Iffigenalp

Gelten Hut SAC	033 765 32 20
Wildhorn Hut SAC	033 733 23 82
Wildstrubel Hut SAC	033 744 33 39

Col du Sanetsch to Iffigenalp

| Cabane des Audannes | 079 310 90 60 |

30 places in a single dormitory

Iffigenalp

There is only one inn here with 14 rooms for 27 people and a dormitory with places for 50, open from the beginning of June until the end of September. Good service and food. If this should be full there is a bus to Lenk where there are several hotels (see below).

| Berghaus Iffigenalp | 033 733 13 33 |

Lenk

A large, but attractive village with all facilities including an excellent open-air swimming pool where you can hire a costume if you don't have one. The food at the Wildstrubel is good and British visitors are especially welcome.

Sporthotel Betelberg ★★★	033 736 33 33
Kreuz ★★★	033 733 13 87
Krone ★★★	033 736 33 44
Wildstrubel ★★★	033 736 31 11

Hotel Simmenfälle	033 733 10 89

At the roadhead below the Simmenfälle

Gasthaus Rezliberg	033 733 12 86

12 places in a dormitory – rather basic

Flueseeli Hut	033 733 21 08

14 places in a dormitory, no warden but there is a wood burning stove and blankets so nothing extra apart from food need be carried.

Engstligenalp

There are two inns here, both near the cable-car station and both offering good value for money.

Hotel Engstligenalp	033 673 22 91

40 beds; 120 places in dormitories

Berghaus Bärtschi	033 673 13 73

18 beds; 55 places in dormitories

Adelboden

Similar in size to Lenk but seems to lack the ambience. There are several hotels but I have no reports on them.

Bristol ★★★	033 673 14 81
Huldi & Waldhaus ★★★	033 673 15 31
Kreuz ★★	033 673 21 21

Gemmipass area

Berghaus Wildstrubel	027 470 12 01
Berghaus Schwarenbach	033 675 12 72

Leukerbad

Many hotels to suit all tastes and pockets. The Weisses Rössli is simple but an extremely good place for bed and breakfast and the Hotel Grichting & Badner-Hof has an excellent table d'hôte.

Alex ★★★	027 472 22 22
Alpenblick ★★★	027 472 70 75
Grichting & Badner-Hof ★★★	027 472 77 11
Derby ★★	027 472 24 72

Gemmi ★ ★	027 470 11 06
Weisses Rössli ★ ★	027 470 33 77
Rinder Hut	027 472 81 30

Places for 58 in rooms with with 4 to 20 beds

Kummenalp
Despite being on a good track from the valley and 45 minutes from the Lauchernalp cable-car station this gasthaus is a simple place with an outside loo and a cold water trough to wash in. But it has enormous charm, a warm welcome, excellent food and fine views of the Dom distantly across the Rhône Valley.

| Gasthaus Kummenalp | 027 939 12 80 |

Lauchernalp
| Hotel Zur Wildi ★ ★ ★ | 027 939 19 89 |
| Berghaus Lauchern | 027 939 12 50 |

Ferden
The Hotel Ambord is a member of the chain of 'Swiss Budget Hotels' and as such offers good value for money.

| Hotel Ambord | 027 939 11 32 |
| Gasthaus Ferdania | 027 939 15 25 |

Kippel
Hotel Lötschberg ★ ★ ★	027 939 13 09
Hotel Petersgrat ★ ★	027 939 18 08
Hotel Bietschhorn	027 939 18 18

Wiler
| Hotel Sporting ★ ★ | 027 939 13 77 |

Opposite the cable-car but that is about its only advantage

Lötschenpass
| Lötschenpass Hut | 027 939 19 81 |

Gfelalp
| Gfelalp | 033 675 11 61 |

Selden

Steinbock	033 675 11 62
Gasthaus Selden	033 675 11 63
Berggasthaus Heimritz	033 675 14 34

Waldhaus

Hotel Waldhaus	033 675 12 75

Kandersteg

The following is a small selection of the many hotels in Kandersteg. The best value is to be found at Zur Post where the owners welcome British visitors. The Bernerhof is also good value for money. The Victoria Ritter used to be popular with British tour operators but nowadays is not as well run as it should be.

Victoria Ritter ★★★★	033 675 80 00
Bernerhof ★★★	033 675 88 75
Alpina ★★	033 675 12 46
Alpenblick ★★	033 675 11 29
Des Alpes ★★	033 675 11 12
Zur Post ★★	033 675 12 58

Appendix B
What to Take

Documents

Passport
Tickets
Insurance
Travellers' cheques
Credit cards
Foreign currency
Driving licence
Alpine club cards

Warm Clothes

Thermal vest
Thermal long-johns
Thermal sweater
Duvet jacket
Balaclava
Thermal gloves

Waterproofs

Light anorak
Over-trousers

Spare Clothes etc

Outer socks
Inner socks
Shirt
Underwear
Long trousers
Hotel shoes and socks
Sleeping bag liner

General Equipment

Maps
Guidebook
Compass
Whistle
GPS
Penknife
Sun block
Camera
Spare battery for camera
Film (as much as you realistically need or spare storage media if you are using a digital camera)
Notebook
Pen
Boot cleaner
Sewing kit
Spare glasses

Toilet Bag

Shower gel
Shaving or other personal requirements
Toothbrush
Toothpaste
Deodorant
Comb
Pack towel

Medical Kit

Padded plaster
Steri-strips
Painkillers
Knife/scissors
Personal medicines

Emergency Gear

Bothy tent or survival bag
Head torch

Food

750ml water bottle
Emergency food such
as dried sausage and
dried apricots

Wear

Boots and socks
Shorts
Shirt
Sun hat
Sun glasses

All these things add up to a rucksack weighing about 11kg but a party of two
or more could share many of the items and a couple should be able to get
away with less than 18kg between them.

Appendix C
Transport

The following timetables were correct at the time of writing. Most of them can be checked on the internet at http://fahrplan.sbb.ch/bin/query.exe/en.

Bex, Villars, Solalex and Les Plans

To start walking from La Barboleusaz there are trains every hour from Villars and Bex between 06:00 and 20:00.

To start from Solalex, there is a bus from Villars via La Barboleusaz which operates from 16 June to 16 September.

Villars	09:45	15:15
La Barboleusaz	09:59	15:24
Solalex	10:10	15:35

Bex (train)	09:23	14:23
La Barboleusaz	09:53	14:53
La Barboleusaz(bus)	09:59	15:24
Solalex	10:10	15:35

To start from Les Plans, there are several buses a day from Bex to Les Plans between 06:45 and 18:45, journey time 25 minutes.

Derborence to Sion

This service runs from the beginning of July to the end of September and could be used if some members of the party did not fancy the Poteu des Etales or if the weather was particularly bad. Overnight accommodation in Sion is fairly easy to find. Hotel Elite is good value and close to the bus and railway station, 027 322 03 27.

Derborence	12:10	16:30
Sion	13:10	17:30
Sion	09:35	14:15
Derborence	10:36	15:16

Sion to Sanetsch

A postbus service between Sion and the Barrage du Sanetsch (dam) runs at weekends from the beginning of July to the end of September and daily from the beginning of July to the middle of August.

Sion	09:15
Coppet	10:03
Plan-Cernet	10:07
Grand Zour	10:12
Sanetsch, hotel	10:37
Col du Sanetsch	10:43
Barrage du Sanetsch	11:03
Barrage du Sanetsch	16:50
Col du Sanetsch	17:00
Sanetsch, hotel	17:06
Grand Zour	17:31
Plan-Cernet	17:36
Coppet	17:40
Sion	18:14

Sanetsch to Gsteig

A cable-car from the dam to Gsteig runs daily from mid June to mid October between 08:30 and 17:00.

Taxi services from Sion

There is a good taxi service in Sion that serves Derborence and Sanetsch. The fare for up to four people is about 90 Swiss Francs. Details are available from 027 322 32 32 or by email: info@fibaval.ch.

Gsteig, Gstaad, Lauenen and Lauenensee

A regular bus service runs between Gsteig and Gstaad from early morning to late evening with at least one bus an hour. There is also a good bus service between Gstaad, Lauenen and Lauenensee.

Iffigenalp and Lenk

A daily bus service runs from mid-June to mid-September. The last bus down from Iffigenalp leaves at 17:45.

Lenk to Simmenfälle

A regular service (roughly once an hour taking 10 minutes). Starting at 07:50 and running throughout the day; the last bus from Simmenfälle is at 17:25.

Engstligenalp and Adelboden

There is an hourly bus service between Adelboden and the cable-car station at Unter dem Birg. The cable-car to Engstligenalp runs between 08:15 and 17:15 (17:45, July and August). Last descent connects with the 18:00 bus to Adelboden.

Leukerbad to Gemmi

Cable-car runs twice an hour between 08:30 and 17:30 from the last week in May to the beginning of July and 08:00 to 18:00 from the beginning of July to the end of October.

Leukerbad to Rinder Hut

Cable-car runs twice an hour between 08:05 and 18:05 from the last week of June to the last week of September.

Wiler to Lauchernalp

Cable-car runs twice an hour between 08:30 and 17:45 (18:10 in July and August).

Selden to Kandersteg

A bus service runs between Selden (Gasthaus Selden) and Kandersteg. The last bus from Selden is at 17:00 (this may not run in bad weather in September). Reservation is necessary, Tel 033 671 11 71/72

Transport

EUROPEAN
WALKING
GUIDES

- Pocket sized guides
- Well-graded routes for families, tours and day-long hikes
- Thoroughly researched and up-to-date
- Topographical route maps and inspirational photography

for the full list of available titles visit
www.cordee.co.uk

Rother Walking Guides are Distributed in the UK by Cordee.
3a De Montfort Street, Leicester, LE1 7HD